Algebra

G E
E
LES

impact

MATHS HOMEWORK

Published by Scholastic Ltd,
Villiers House,
Clarendon Avenue,
Leamington Spa,
Warwickshire CV32 5PR

© **1994 Scholastic Ltd**
Text © 1994 University of North London
Enterprises Ltd
2 3 4 5 6 7 8 9   7 8 9 0 1 2 3

Activities by the IMPACT Project at the University
of North London, collated and rewritten by Ruth
Merttens and Ros Leather

Editor Jo Saxelby-Jennings
Assistant editor Joanne Boden
Designer Lucy Smith
Series designer Anna Oliwa
Illustrations Derek Matthews
Cover illustration Roger Wade Walker

Designed using Aldus Pagemaker; processed by
Pages Bureau, Leamington Spa
Artwork by Pages Bureau, Leamington Spa
Printed in Great Britain by Ebenezer Baylis,
Worcester

British Library Cataloguing-in-Publication Data
A catalogue record for this book is available from the British
Library.

ISBN 0-590-53160-3

Algebra

impact
CONTENTS

Algebra

impact
CONTENTS

impact
INTRODUCTION

This series of IMPACT books is designed to help you run a non-traditional homework scheme. Through the use of take-home maths activities, children can share maths with a parent/carer in the context of the home. The results of these activities then feed back into the classwork at school.

IMPACT works through the following processes:
- Teachers plan their maths for the next few weeks as usual and consider which parts might usefully be done at home.
- Teachers look through selected activities which fit in with what they are planning.
- The activities are photocopied and sent home with the children every week or fortnight.
- The results of each activity are brought back into the classroom by the children and form part of the following week's classwork.

In practice this process will be slightly different in each classroom and in each school. Teachers may adapt it to fit their own way of working and the ethos of the school in which they work.

Most schools send out IMPACT activities fortnightly, although some do send it weekly. There is some evidence to suggest that weekly activities get a slightly better response and help to raise standards more effectively than

fortnightly, but this is not conclusive. The important point is that each teacher should feel comfortable with how often the IMPACT activities are used in his/her class.

Planning

When you, the teacher, are looking at your work and deciding what maths, roughly speaking, you plan to be doing over the next few weeks, all that is necessary is to consider which parts may usefully be done or practised at home. It is helpful if, over a period of time, a range of activities are chosen in order to vary the mathematical experience in the home and the type and amount of follow-up required in class.

The activities tend to fall into three broad categories:
- Activities which practise a skill – these are useful in that they can be followed up in the routine classwork the children are doing. They must be carefully selected by the teacher according to the level of the children.
- Activities which collect data – these lead into work on data-handling and representation.
- Activities in which the children measure something – this produces an object or some measurements to be used later in class.

The activities in this book are divided into three sections according to age: Reception, Year 1 and Year 2. There are two pages of teachers' notes relating to the individual activities at the beginning of each sections.

Links to National Curriculum Programmes of Study for Using and Applying Mathematics and for Number are given in each section of teachers' notes. A breakdown of the Programmes of Study appropriate to the ability of children in that year is given.

Details of how these relate to the curricula in Scotland and Northern Ireland are given on page 128.

Working with parents

It is important for the success of IMPACT that the activities taken home are seen by the parents to be maths. We always suggest, at least until IMPACT is up and running and parents' confidence in it is well established, that activities are chosen which have a clearly mathematical purpose.

Save the more 'wacky' activities until later! You will get a much better response if parents believe that what they are doing is maths.

Each activity contains a note to parents which explains the purpose of the activity and how they can best help. The IMPACT activities should be accompanied by an IMPACT diary, enabling parents and children to make their comments. See page 128 for details.

Making the most of IMPACT

The quickest way to reduce the number of children who share maths at home is to ignore or be negative about the work that they bring back into school. When the children come running into the classroom, tripping over the string which went twice round their cat, it is difficult to welcome them all individually but it is crucial that the activities done at home are followed up in classwork. The nature and type of this follow-up work depends very much upon the nature of the activity, and specific suggestions are made in the teachers' notes. However, some general points apply:
- Number activities, such as games, can often be repeated in a more formalised way in the classwork. For example, if the children have been playing a dice game, throwing two dice and adding the totals,

they can continue to do this in the classroom, but this time they can record all the 'sums' in their maths books. This applies to any skills-practice activity.
- Data-collecting activities, of any description, need to be followed up by allowing the children to work together in small groups to collate, analyse and represent their joint data. This will inevitably involve children in a discussion as to how their data was obtained, and any problems they encountered while obtaining it.
- If the children have made or measured something at home, the information or the object needs to be used as part of the resulting classwork. This will not be too difficult since this type of activity is selected by the teacher precisely in order to provide the measurements or shapes for use in class.

The implication of this is that it is wise to select a variety of activities to send home. No teacher wants to drown in data, nor do they want all the IMPACT activities to result in more routine number work. Some activities generate lots of follow-up while others simply require minimal follow-up – sometimes just a discussion about who won and who lost, and how many times people played the game.

Many of the activities can lead to an attractive display or enable the teacher to make a class book. Such a book does not have to be 'grand'. It can be simply five or six sheets large sheets of sugar paper folded in the middle and stitched/stapled with the children's work mounted inside it. The children love these books, and they make a fine record of their work. An IMPACT display board in the school entrance hall gives parents a sense that their work at home is appreciated.
For further details of IMPACT see page 128.

Teachers' Notes
RECEPTION

All these activities provide opportunities for children to use and apply their mathematical skills outside the context of the classroom. This means that every activity will address some aspects of the 'Using and Applying' part of the Programme of Study (was AT1). Commonly children may be expected to do the following whilst sharing IMPACT activity:
● use and apply mathematics in practical tasks and in real–life problems,
● find their own way through tasks, explaining what they do as they go,
● develop their own strategies and discuss these with others, and
● give and follow instructions, and talk about their results.

These are important parts of 'Using and Applying' mathematics. The evidence from OFSTED and other reports now clearly demonstrates that IMPACT can have a marked affect in this area of children's mathematical development. The activities in this book also address aspects of the Programme of Study for Number, specifically in relation to number patterns.

In particular, this section utilises the following skills:
● recognising and using simple repetitive patterns, including many counting patterns,
● recognising and using simple adding and taking away patterns,
● starting to recognise even and odd numbers – up to ten,
● recognising line symmetry, and

● recognising simple sequences.

A bracelet of beads Ask the children to read their patterns. Have any children made the same pattern? The could arrange themselves into sets with the same pattern. Their bracelets could be used for shopping activities in a class shop or to sell at the school fête.

Design a headband Encourage the children to read out their pattern. The headbands could be displayed with captions and questions, such as 'How many patterns fit around Mary's headband? How many children have used all the shapes on their headband?'

A plate for teddy The plates could be displayed and questions asked, such as. 'How many teddies have they used? How many repeated patterns are there around the plate? How many children have used the same patterns?' The children could design a border of various–sized teddy bears to go round the edge of their display: a daddy bear, a mummy bear, a baby bear and so on; or, a daddy bear, a mummy bear, two baby bears and so on.

Design a plate for a new baby The children could share their plate patterns. They could play a circle game. The children could turn round and one child reads out one pattern repeat from his plate. The plate is then hidden and the other children try to carry on the pattern. Check if they are right. Repeat with other plates.

PE pattern The children can play the game 'Follow–my–leader' in PE or on the playground, chanting the patterns that they make as they travel. They could go on to work in pairs, using both their patterns to make a larger sequence of movements. Can they find ways of recording their patterns? These can be displayed and used in other PE lessons.

A bedroom border The children can arrange their patterns on to a long strip of paper. This will make an interesting border

to go around the home corner. Ask the children to count the pattern: how many blue rabbits are there, for example? Can they count the rabbits' ears in twos?

Sitting at the table The table arrangements could be used for counting activities. How many squares are there? How many blue rabbits are there? The children could draw plates and mugs for each rabbit, making sure they keep the colour pattern. This activity could be extended to make a display of different shaped tables with other rabbits arranged around them. The work that the children brought from home could be used as a border to this display.

A wallpaper pattern The children could investigate how many squares they can find in the big square. How many of them are coloured? The children could look at books to find repeating patterns. Some of which could be reproduced by the children or they could design their own patterns based on a familiar story. All the ideas could be displayed and questions asked.

Shape mobile The children can talk about their own mobiles. Has anyone made the same arrangement? Has anyone used the same colours for their shapes? These mobiles will make excellent displays above tables in the classroom and help the children with shape recognition. Shape words could be added to the mobiles.

Music patterns The children can form groups where the syllables in their names match. Each group can make their sound patterns. These could be accompanied by percussion instruments. The children may like to experiment with pictures to represent their sounds. The children could try and join some of the sounds together to make longer sequences.

Growing then shrinking The patterns the children have discussed could make a border around a display. They could make a similar pattern using shapes made by

drawing round their shoes. Groups of children could use Multilink cubes to make growing and shrinking patterns, such as: 2, 4, 6, 4, 2, 4, 6 and so on, or 2, 4, 6, 6, 4, 2, 2, 4, 6, and so on.

Patterned snake The children could estimate and measure their snakes using a variety of non–standard units. The snakes could be displayed with other symmetrical patterns, such as string patterns or blot pictures of butterflies or insects.

Block patterns Pairs of children could continue the patterns that their friends have made. All the patterns could be displayed in various sets around the class: repeating patterns and growing and shrinking patterns for example.

Symmetrical butterfly The children may like to make other symmetrical patterns, such as blot pictures or string patterns. Let them cut half pictures of faces from magazines and try to complete the faces by drawing and colouring the other side. These symmetrical patterns would make an excellent display.

Christmas chains This idea can be used with real strips of paper as Christmas decorations. The children could experiment with hanging bell or lantern shapes at regular intervals on their festive chains – a good way of decorating the classroom while having fun!

Hoops Encourage children to use bricks to create more complicated interlocking patterns. They could work in pairs or small groups to complete this activity. Their patterns could be recorded using strips of paper and coloured squares and displayed in a class book.

Domino patterns Let the children work in pairs to arrange the dominoes in different patterns: for example, 6 and 0, 6 and 1, 6 and 2 and so on. Perhaps they could make paper dominoes with random spots and discuss which dominoes are the easiest to use and why.

The Three Bears Many books have interesting patterns and borders – the children may like to investigate these first. Then their pictures could be displayed in a class book near a large picture of 'Goldilocks and the Three Bears'. This picture could be bordered by a pattern designed by the children.

Number chains This activity will help the children to count in twos. Sit them in a circle, each with a number (start with 1) which they must remember. When they are familiar with the sequence, they could play a simplified version of 'Fizz Buzz'.

Dice puzzle This is an excellent practice for finding number bonds. The idea can be extended to other numbers by using Cuisenaire rods or joining cubes. Give each child in the group a different number (such as 2 or 6). Then they must find partners to make a combined total number (such as 8).

Traffic lights Make large traffic lights from junk to display the light sequence. The children could investigate why the sequence works in this particular order (using the Highway Code). This investigation could lead to other work on road signs and road safety.

Flowers How many different ways of arranging the petals have the children discovered? Can they group their flowers into different arrangements and explain what they are? These could be grouped in different sets to produce a wall display in the form of a garden picture.

Playing cards – odds and evens The children could work in groups to arrange the playing cards in pairs that total either odd or even numbers. They might like to investigate what happens when two odd numbers are added or two even numbers or one of each. Is there a rule? These investigations could be displayed with some large playing cards showing examples of each rule.

Buttons – odds and evens The children could work in pairs to investigate ways of arranging Multilink to show the difference between odd and even numbers. The snakes that they made at home could be displayed in a class book and the colour patterns produced could be investigated.

Design your own dice The children may like to write the rules about what happens when odd, and then when even, numbers are added. These could be displayed with some of their totals. The investigation could be continued by halving even numbers and discovering if there is a pattern – is the result always even?

Your age – odd or even The children could play a game in PE making this pattern: one child = no partner (odd); two children = one pair (even); three children = one pair, one left over (odd); four children = two pairs (even) and so on. They could be encouraged to verbalise this as the pattern grows. Can they start with the big number and count backwards, sitting down one at a time as they say their number out loud. They might like to group themselves, or they could be arranged in pairs, to demonstrate even numbers.

Dominoes – odds and evens The children could work in groups to sort the dominoes into two sets, one set of even-totalled dominoes and one set of odd-totalled dominoes. Arrange each set in order of size. Is there a pattern? What do the children notice if the ordered sets are placed next to each other? The children could make their own dominoes and place them in the pattern of their choice.

Eating raisins Play 'Pairs' using shoes: six children arrange their shoes in pairs; 12 is an even number. What happens if one shoe is mislaid? (You get an odd shoe, so 11 is an odd number.) The children may like to draw themselves and stick their pictures in pairs to represent their group. These could be displayed and questions

asked, such as, 'Are all our groups an even number?' Which groups are odd?'

Odd or even–numbered family Arrange the family pictures into two sets: odds and evens. Within these sets, the children could arrange the family members into size order. These could be displayed as a pictogram and questions asked. 'Do we have more odd families than even families? Is our largest family odd or even?'

My bed The children can group themselves into sets of odd and even numbers of feet needed to measure the bed. Why are there different measurements? Tell the story about the 'Carpenter's apprentice'. The king ordered a bed for his wife, the carpenter measured the bed using his feet and wrote the instructions for his apprentice. Can the children guess what happened?

What can you see? Put the children's drawing of the objects that they see on their journeys to and from school in a class book. Perhaps groups could be taken on a short walk. Each group could remember four significant objects. A map could be drawn and their objects placed in the correct positions. The children could take turns to say..'As I walked along the street, I saw a …'.

Boiling an egg The children can stick their instructions into a class book. Do all the instructions have the same order. You may like to make a jelly. The children can help you to write the instructions which can be cut up and arranged in order. They could make illustrations to accompany the instructions. These could be displayed with their egg book.

Pairs You will need two sets of 0 – 10 cards. Ask each child to take a card and then find a partner to total ten. Can each partner explain their total? Perhaps they could arrange themselves in a pattern. Cards with numbers up to 20 could be made and arranged in pairs to make a

pattern; for example 15 + 5 or 16 + 4 and so on. Can they discover more patterns?

Three cards to make 10 The children could investigate the patterns for making 10 with three cards, beginning with 9 + 1 + 0 and then 8 + 1 + 1. What do they think will come next? The children could paint shapes on to individual small sheets of paper to represent cards. These could then be arranged and displayed in their patterns. Each day the children and teacher can turn over two cards. Can the children say what the third card will need to be?

Ten LEGO pieces The children can learn songs like 'Ten fat sausages' with each child holding a number card, so that they can see how the number of sausages reduces by two each time. Play circle games. For example, ten children stand up. How many must sit down to leave 4? Say the sum, '10 take away 6 leaves 4.'

Penny patterns The children may like to work in pairs to reproduce their patterns using Multilink. Can they make more patterns with Multilink? How many can be made? How do they know that they have made them all? Can they be arranged in sets? How many sets are there? Their work can be recorded on to squared paper and displayed with the sorting criteria.

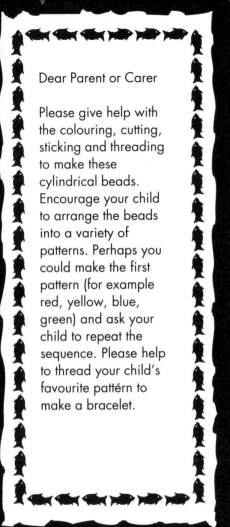

_____and

child

_____

helper(s)

_____

did this activity together

A bracelet of beads

YOU WILL NEED: four different coloured pencils or felt-tipped pens, a knitting needle, some sticky tape or adhesive and some thread.

● Colour in each of the strips on the accompanying sheet with one of your colours and then cut the strips out carefully.

● Wind each of the strips around the knitting needle and stick the end of the strip to prevent it uncurling. Slip it off the needle to make a bead.

● Arrange your beads in a pattern and then thread them to make a bracelet.

● Bring your bracelet into school.

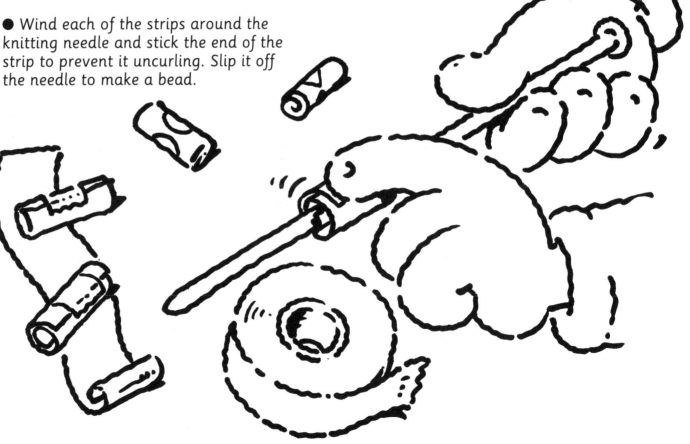

impact MATHS HOMEWORK

A bracelet of beads

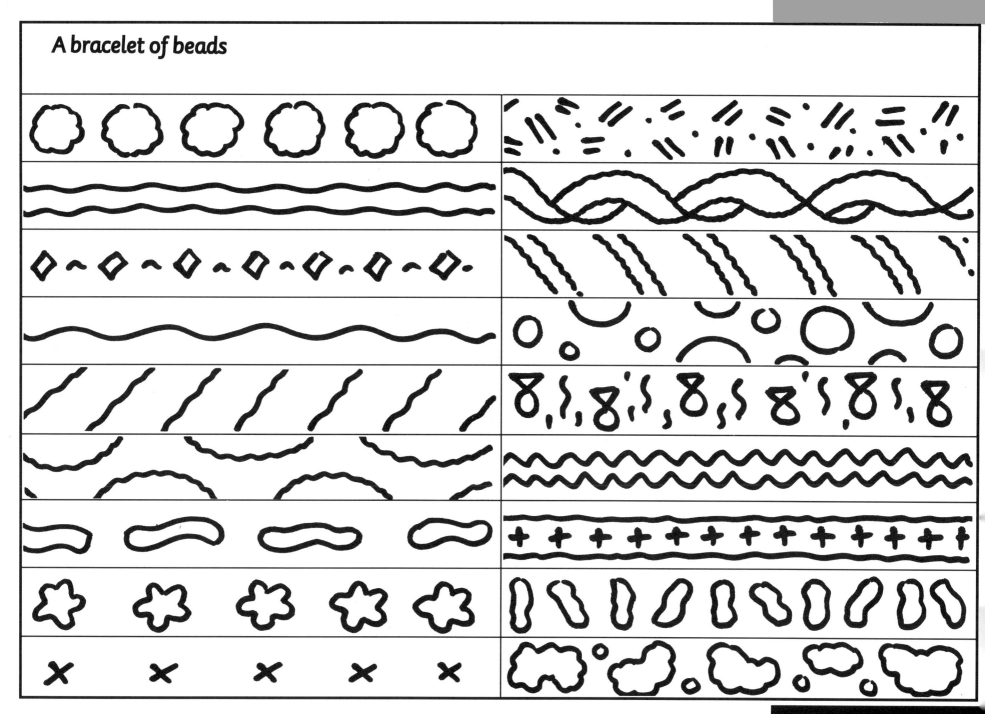

Dear Parent or Carer

Please encourage your child to colour the shapes before cutting them out (give help with the cutting too, if it is required). Try different pattern arrangements, such as: red circle, blue square, red circle, blue square...; one yellow circle, two blue squares, one yellow circle, two blue squares, and so on. Stick your child's favourite pattern on to their headband – you may not require all the shapes.

________________________and

child

____

helper(s)

____

did this activity together

Design a headband

- Make a headband that will fit your head.
- Use the circles and squares on this page to make a pattern around your headband. Remember to colour your shapes carefully. Use one colour for circles and a different colour for squares.
- Please bring your headband into school.

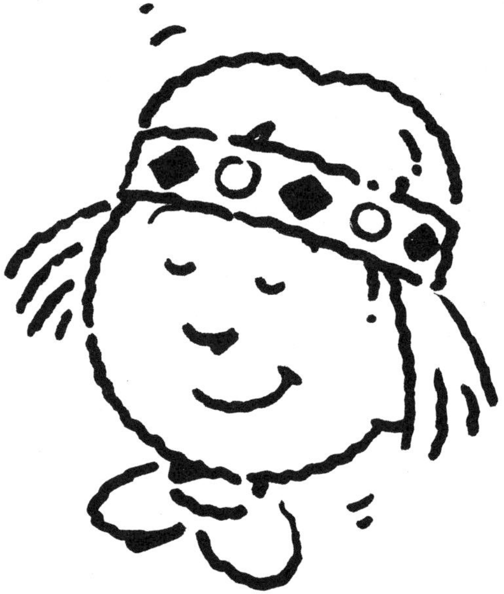

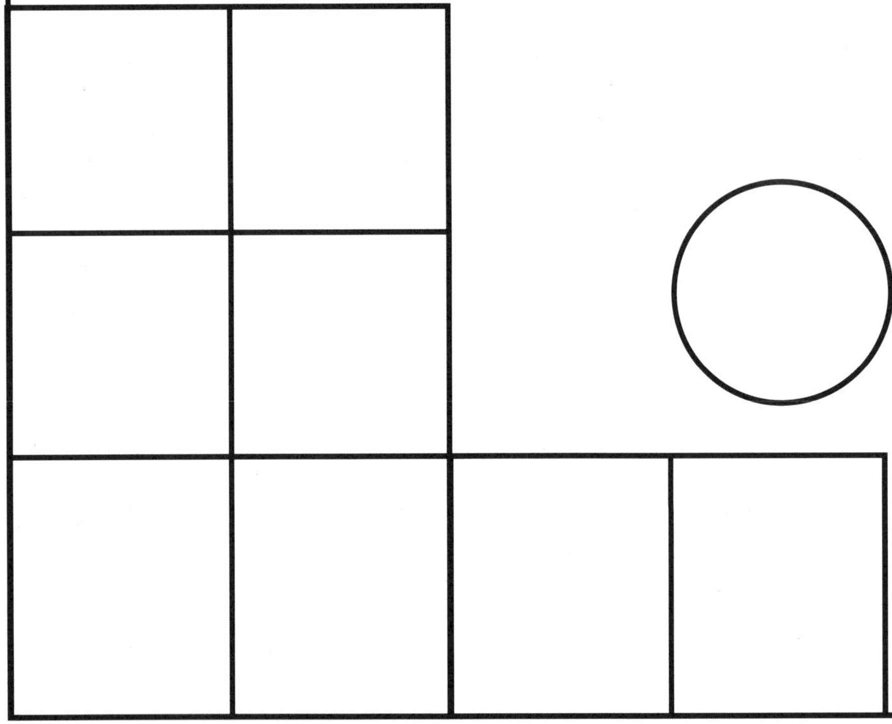

A plate for teddy

● Please look at the patterns around the edges of your plates at home.

● Colour the teddies at the bottom of the page using two colours.

● Cut out the squares and arrange the teddies in a pattern around the edge of the plate.

● Stick the teddies on carefully and bring your beautiful plate to school.

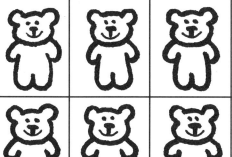

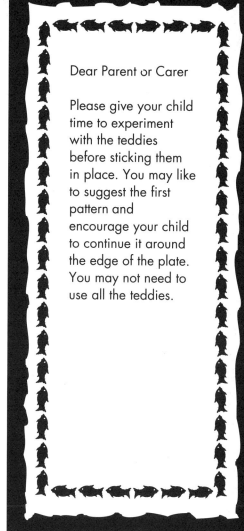

Dear Parent or Carer

Please give your child time to experiment with the teddies before sticking them in place. You may like to suggest the first pattern and encourage your child to continue it around the edge of the plate. You may not need to use all the teddies.

_____and

child

_____

helper(s)

_____

did this activity together

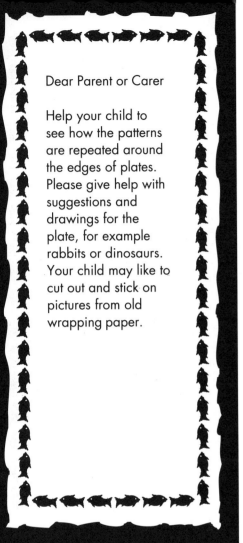

Dear Parent or Carer

Help your child to see how the patterns are repeated around the edges of plates. Please give help with suggestions and drawings for the plate, for example rabbits or dinosaurs. Your child may like to cut out and stick on pictures from old wrapping paper.

_____and

child

_____

helper(s)

_____

did this activity together

Design a plate for a new baby

● Look at the patterns around your plates at home.

● Design a pattern to go round the edge of a plate for a new baby.

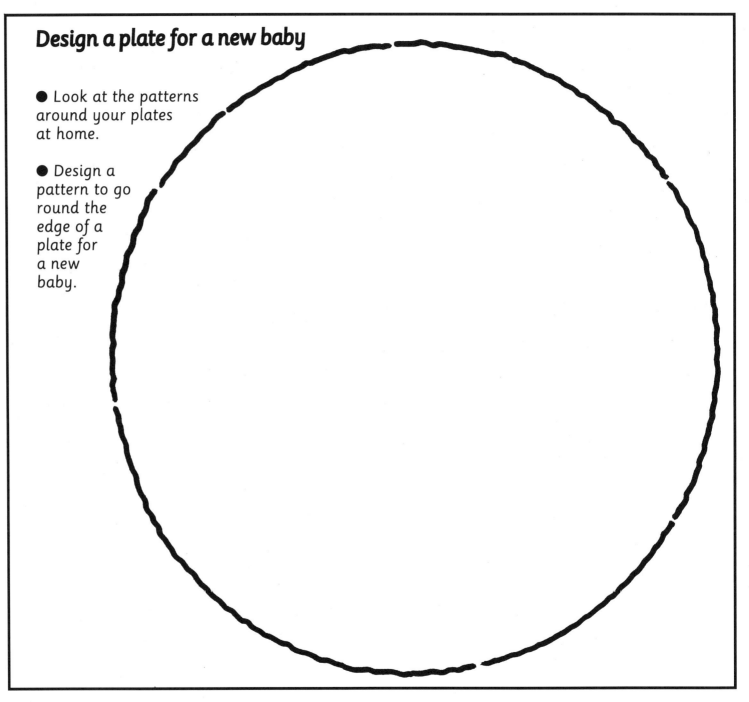

impact MATHS HOMEWORK

PE pattern

- Plan a PE pattern.

- Use two hops, three jumps with feet together and two other jumps (long jumps, high jumps, zigzag jumps and so on) to make an interesting shape with your pattern.

- Repeat the sequence three times.

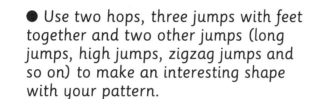

- Try to remember your pattern to show in school. Perhaps you could draw a picture of your pattern.

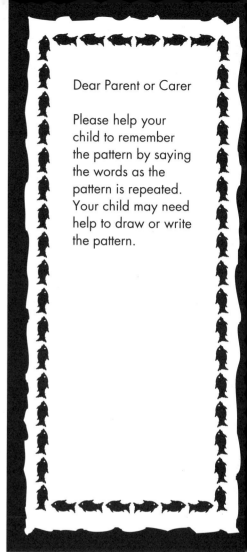

Dear Parent or Carer

Please help your child to remember the pattern by saying the words as the pattern is repeated. Your child may need help to draw or write the pattern.

_____and

child

_____

helper(s)

_____

did this activity together

A bedroom border

● Please colour the rabbits below carefully.

● Colour your big rabbits blue, your medium rabbits yellow and your small rabbits green.

● Cut out the rectangles and stick your rabbits on to a strip of paper in a pattern.

● Please bring your rabbit border to school.

impact MATHS HOMEWORK

Sitting at the table

● Colour the rabbits at the bottom of the page carefully using four colours.

● Cut out the rabbits in their rectangles and arrange them in a pattern around the table.

● Please bring your arrangement in to school.

Dear Parent or Carer

Please help your child to cut out the rectangles. Give your child time to arrange the rabbits around the table before sticking them on.

_____and

child

_____

helper(s)

_____

did this activity together

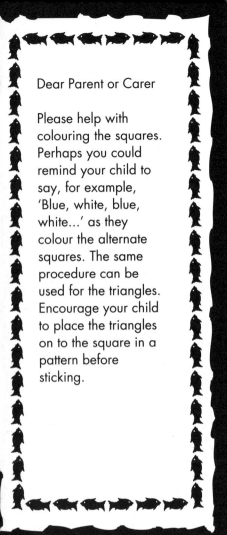
_____and

child

_____

helper(s)

_____

did this activity together

A wallpaper pattern

● Using only one colour,
colour every other
square.

● How many coloured
squares are there?

● Colour the triangles
and cut them out. Stick
them on to the squares
to make a nice pattern.

impact MATHS HOMEWORK

Shape mobile

- Colour the shapes carefully and then cut them out.

- Colour the other side of each shape to match the first side.

- Arrange the shapes into a pattern. Ask someone at home to help you thread your favourite pattern to make a mobile.

- Bring your mobile into school.

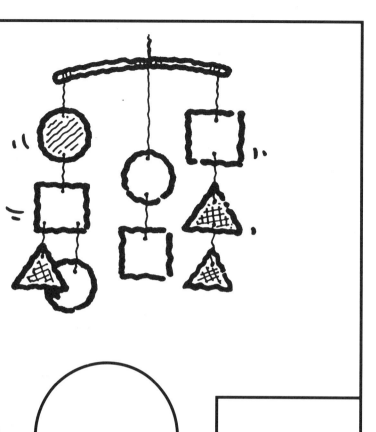

_____and

child

_____

helper(s)

_____

did this activity together

Dear Parent or Carer

Please help your child to experiment with clapping the syllables in their names and other family names. Try other hand/finger sounds to match the syllables in these names. Please help your child to record the sound pattern for their name.

_____and

child

_____

helper(s)

_____

did this activity together

Music patterns

● Use your hands to make different sounds – rubbing, clapping or clicking.

● Can you make a sound pattern for your name? For example:

Ma – ry   Smith

● Perhaps you could draw a picture or write your sound pattern below.

impact MATHS HOMEWORK

Growing then shrinking

● Carefully colour the flowers opposite and then cut out the rectangles. Use them to make a pattern.

● Can you make the flowers in your pattern get bigger and then smaller?

● Stick your pattern carefully on to a strip of paper and bring it into school.

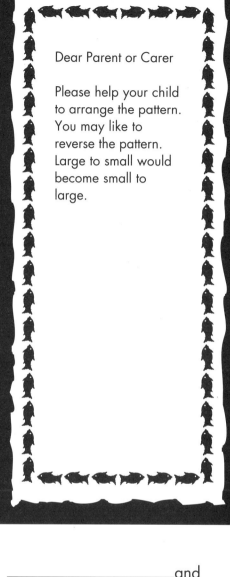
_____and

child

_____

helper(s)

_____

did this activity together

impact MATHS HOMEWORK

Dear Parent or Carer

Your child will be designing a symmetrical pattern. Talk about other symmetrical objects, including our bodies, cars, butterflies and so on.

_____and

child

_____

helper(s)

_____

did this activity together

Patterned snake

● Can you draw triangles on the opposite side of the snake to match the side already drawn for you?

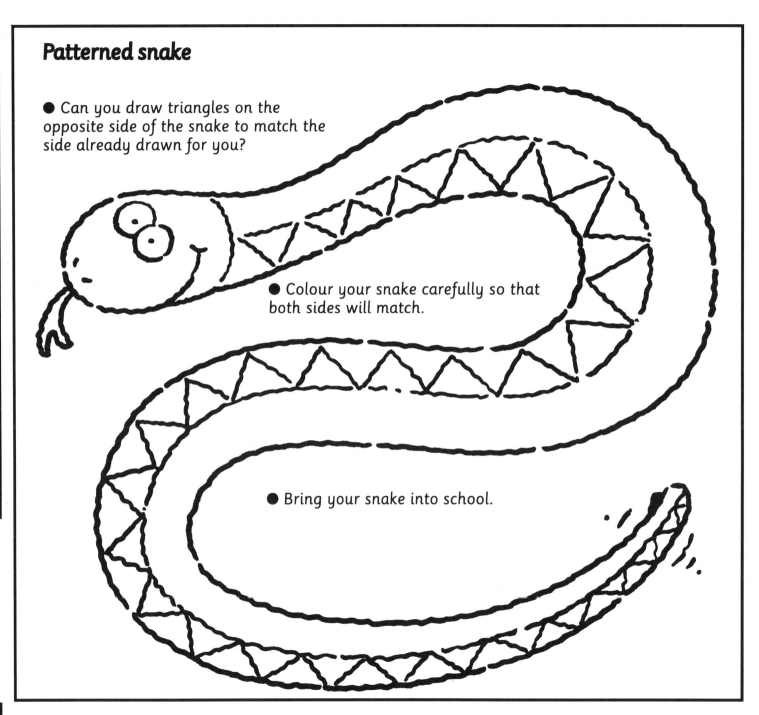

● Colour your snake carefully so that both sides will match.

● Bring your snake into school.

impact MATHS HOMEWORK

Block patterns

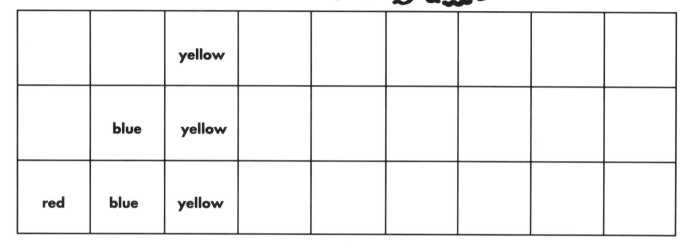

● Colour in this pattern carefully. Can you carry on the pattern?

		yellow						
	blue	yellow						
red	blue	yellow						

● Use these squares to design a coloured pattern for your friend to continue in class.

Dear Parent or Carer

There are several ways of continuing this pattern. Please give your child time and be prepared for surprises!

_____and
child

_____
helper(s)

_____

did this activity together

Symmetrical butterfly

● Cut out the small shapes carefully and stick them on to match the other side of the butterfly.

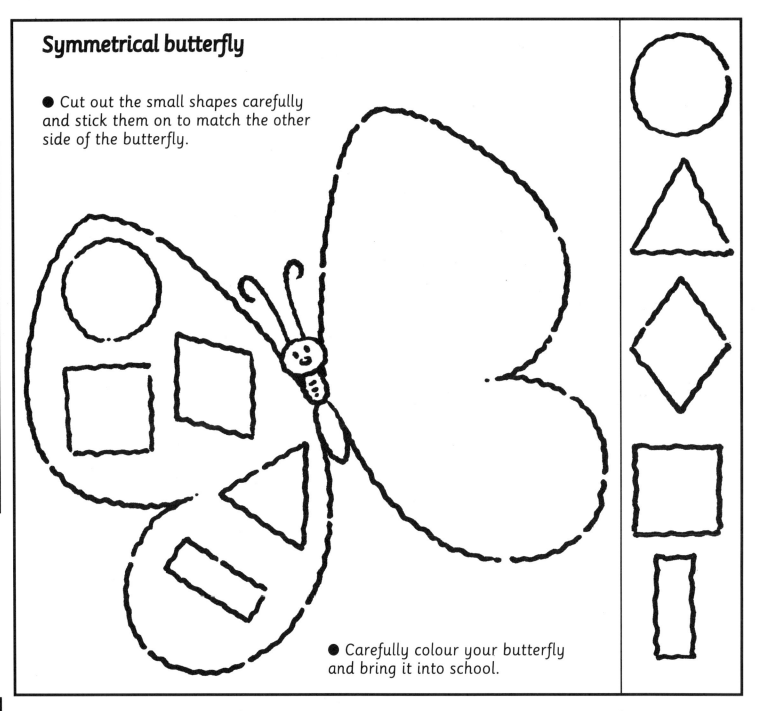

● Carefully colour your butterfly and bring it into school.

impact MATHS HOMEWORK

Christmas chains

- Colour the first two rings red.

- Colour ring number 3 in yellow.

- Keep counting and colouring in a pattern. Think carefully before you start.

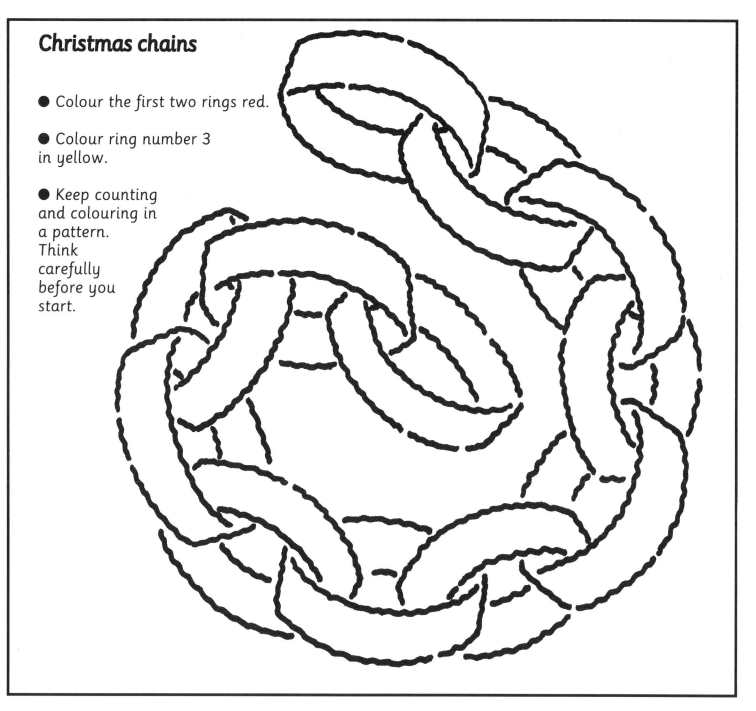

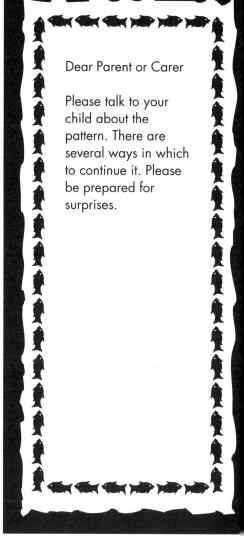
_____and

child

_____

helper(s)

_____

did this activity together

Hoops

● Colour in the squares carefully to make a pattern.

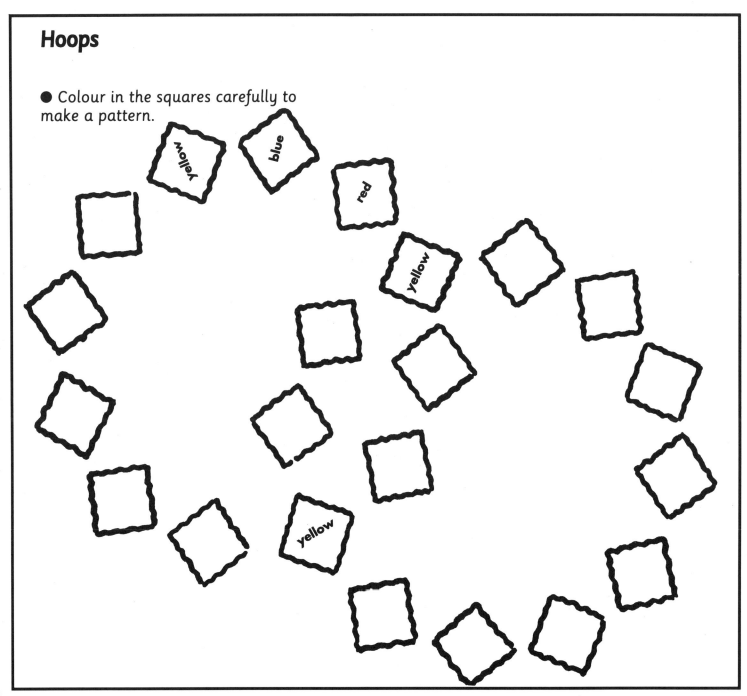

Domino patterns

YOU WILL NEED: a set of dominoes.

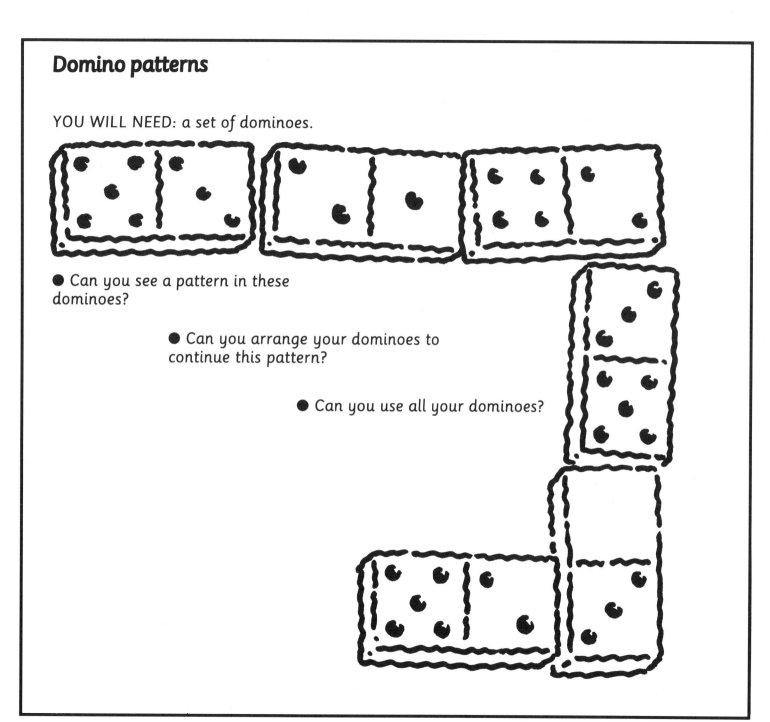

● Can you see a pattern in these dominoes?

● Can you arrange your dominoes to continue this pattern?

● Can you use all your dominoes?

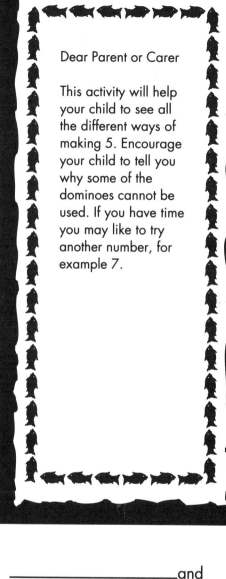

Dear Parent or Carer

This activity will help your child to see all the different ways of making 5. Encourage your child to tell you why some of the dominoes cannot be used. If you have time you may like to try another number, for example 7.

_____and

child

_____

helper(s)

_____

did this activity together

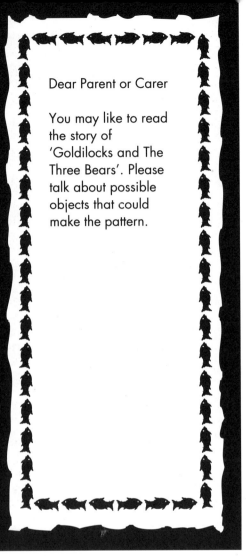
The Three Bears

● What patterned border do you think
an illustrator would put round the edge
of this picture?

● Draw in your favourite idea.

impact MATHS HOMEWORK

Number chains

- Can you continue this number chain?

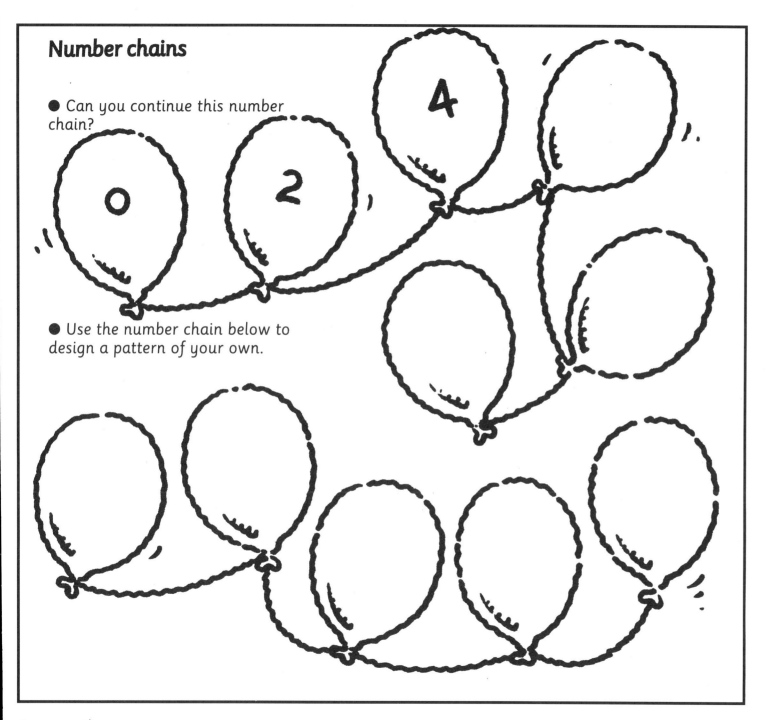

- Use the number chain below to design a pattern of your own.

Dear Parent or Carer

Please help your child to count in twos. It is often helpful to say the missing number in a whisper and the written one loudly.

_____ and

child

_____

helper(s)

_____

did this activity together

Dice puzzle

● Hold the opposite sides of a dice.

● Write down the numbers you are touching and add them.

● Do this until you have all the possible arrangements.

● What do you notice?

● Ask someone to play the following game with you. Throw the dice, can you say which number is hidden? Can you always find the answer?

impact MATHS HOMEWORK

Traffic lights

YOU WILL NEED to find a safe place to look at traffic lights.

● Carefully colour in these pictures to show the patterns of lights that you see.

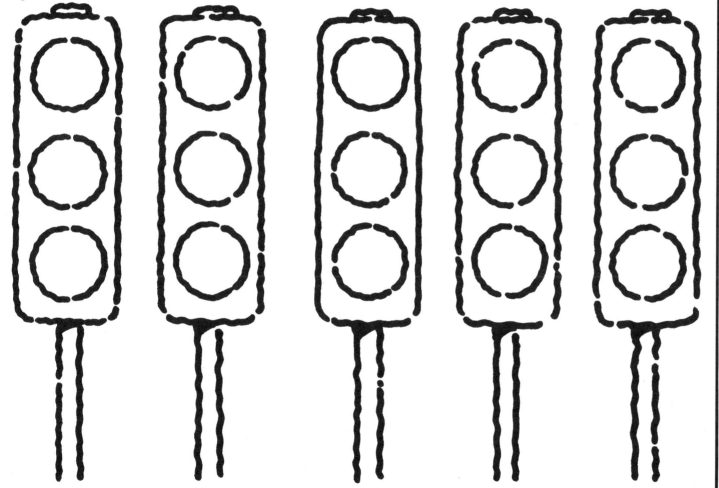

Dear Parent or Carer

Please take your child to look at traffic lights. If you have time you may like to look at other lights, such as Pelican Crossings.

_____and

child

_____

helper(s)

_____

did this activity together

Flowers

● Each flower has six petals. For each flower, use three colours. Colour two petals for each flower in each colour.

● In how many ways can you arrange the petals around the centre?

● Bring your beautiful flowers into school.

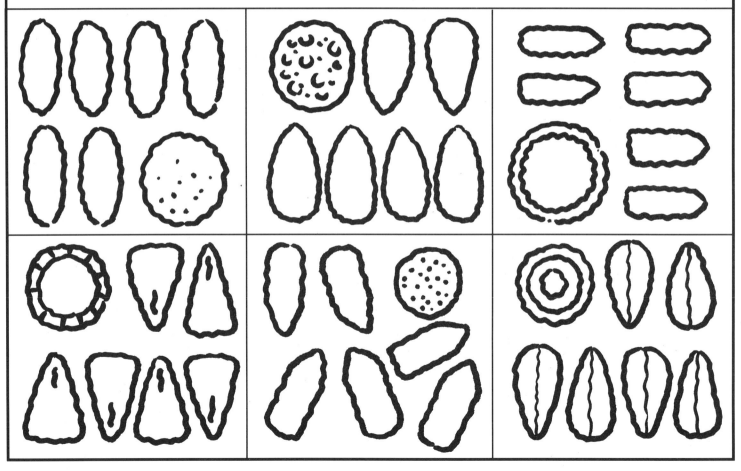

impact MATHS HOMEWORK

Playing cards – odds and evens

YOU WILL NEED: all the red cards from 1–10 laid out face down.

● This game needs two players – one is 'odds' and the other 'evens'.

● Take it in turns to pick up two cards.

● If the total is odd, you may keep them if you are the 'odds' person. If not, return them.

● Take turns, the person with the most pairs is the winner.

_____and

child

_____

helper(s)

_____

did this activity together

Buttons – odds and evens

YOU WILL NEED: at least 20 buttons (or pieces of LEGO or small bricks) and red and yellow crayons.

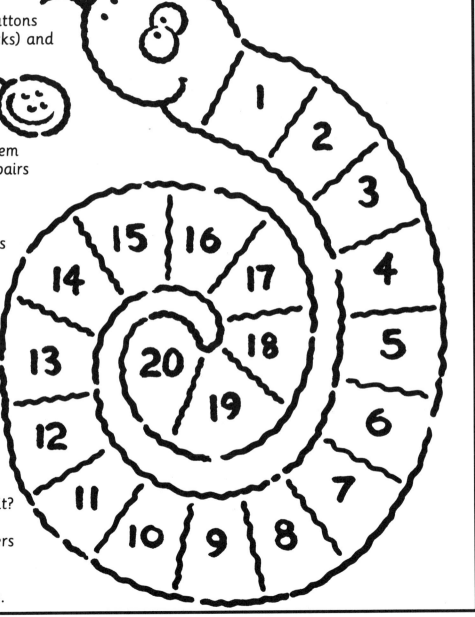

● Take some buttons, count them carefully and arrange them in pairs (twos).

● Is every button in a pair? If they are, the number of buttons is even. For example, 6 is an even number, so colour it yellow on the snake.

● Try other numbers of buttons.

● If the number of buttons cannot be arranged in pairs it is odd – colour it red on the snake.

● Try all the numbers on the snake. What has happened to it?

● Can you read the red numbers in order?

● Now try the yellow numbers.

Design your own dice

YOU WILL NEED: two cubes or bricks and some sticky numbers.

● To make an even-numbered dice, stick red numbers 2, 4, 6, 8, 10 and 12 on to your cube.

● To make an odd-numbered dice, stick blue numbers 1, 3, 5, 7, 9 and 11 on to your cube.

● Throw your red dice twice and add up the scores. Do this several times, make a list of your sums opposite. Are your answers odd or even?

● Use your blue dice in the same way. Are your answers odd or even?

● Now try throwing both dice once and finding the total. Are your answers odd or even?

● Can you explain the answers? Is there a rule?

Dear Parent or Carer

Please encourage your child to start adding with the larger number. For example, if you throw an 8 and a 10, start with the 10 and add on the 8. You may need to remind your child about the difference between an odd and an even number. Try using buttons, if the number of buttons can be put into pairs it is an even number; if not, it is odd.

_____and

child

_____

helper(s)

_____

did this activity together

_____and

child

_____

helper(s)

_____

did this activity together

Your age – odd or even

● Is your age an odd or an even number?

● Draw the right number of candles on to each cake. Try to draw your candles in pairs.

● Are you in an odd or an even year?

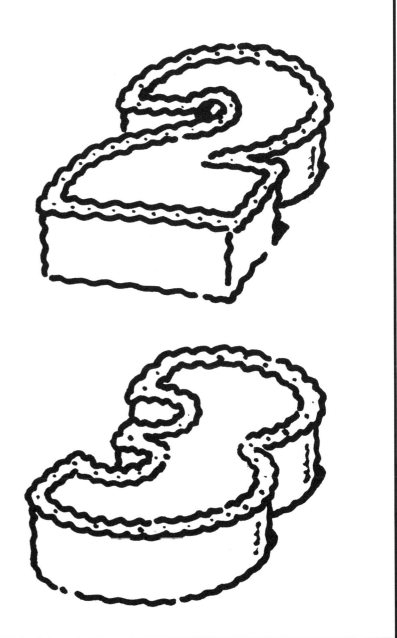

● What were you last year?

● What will you be next year?

impact MATHS HOMEWORK

Your age – odd or even

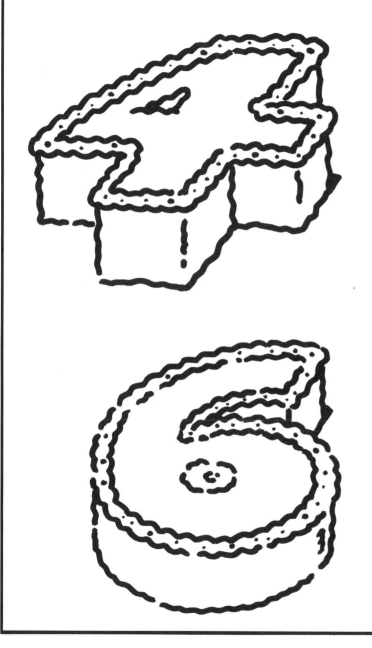

Dominoes – odds and evens

YOU WILL NEED: a set of dominoes.

● Take turns with someone to continue this domino pattern.

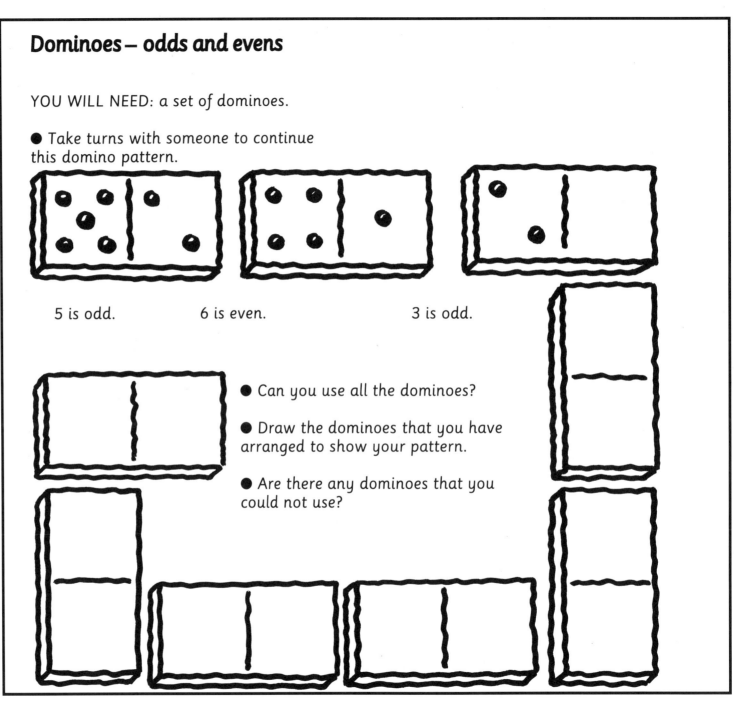

5 is odd.   6 is even.   3 is odd.

● Can you use all the dominoes?

● Draw the dominoes that you have arranged to show your pattern.

● Are there any dominoes that you could not use?

impact MATHS HOMEWORK

Eating raisins

YOU WILL NEED: ten raisins and a partner.

● Arrange your raisins in pairs, each person eats one raisin.

● Make a chart to show how many are left each time you both take a raisin. Are the numbers odd or even?

● Try the game again. This time you will need 18 raisins and three people to play the game.

● Arrange your raisins in pairs. Every time the three of you take a raisin, how many are left?

● Record your results. Are the answers odd or even? Can you explain what has happened?

Dear Parent or Carer

Please encourage your child to talk about odd and even numbers. If a raisin has a partner (is in a pair) it is even, otherwise it is odd.

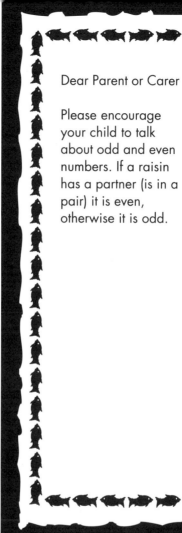

_____and

child

_____

helper(s)

_____

did this activity together

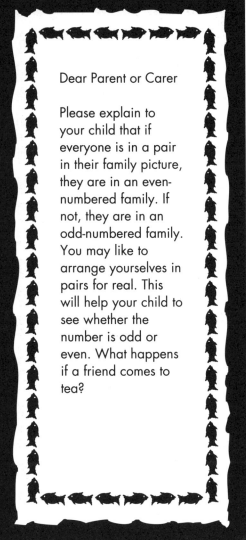
Odd or even-numbered family

● On another piece of paper, draw everyone in your family and cut out your pictures carefully.

● Arrange your pictures in pairs and stick them on to the frame below.

● Bring your family picture to school.

impact MATHS HOMEWORK

My bed

● Measure the length of your bed with your feet.

● Have you used an odd number or an even number of feet?

● Ask other family members to try.

● Make a chart to show each person's measurement and whether it is an odd or an even number.

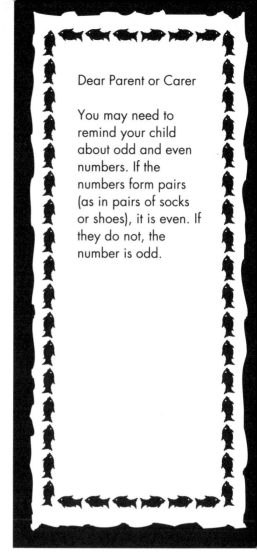

Dear Parent or Carer

You may need to remind your child about odd and even numbers. If the numbers form pairs (as in pairs of socks or shoes), it is even. If they do not, the number is odd.

_____and

child

_____

helper(s)

_____

did this activity together

_____and

child

_____

helper(s)

_____

did this activity together

What can you see?

● Try to remember four things that you pass every morning on your way to school. Make sure that you remember them in the order that you see them.

● What happens to the things you saw this morning on your homeward journey?

● Can you draw the four things you saw this morning and this afternoon? Make sure that you draw them in the right orders.

On the way to school

On the way home

What can you see?

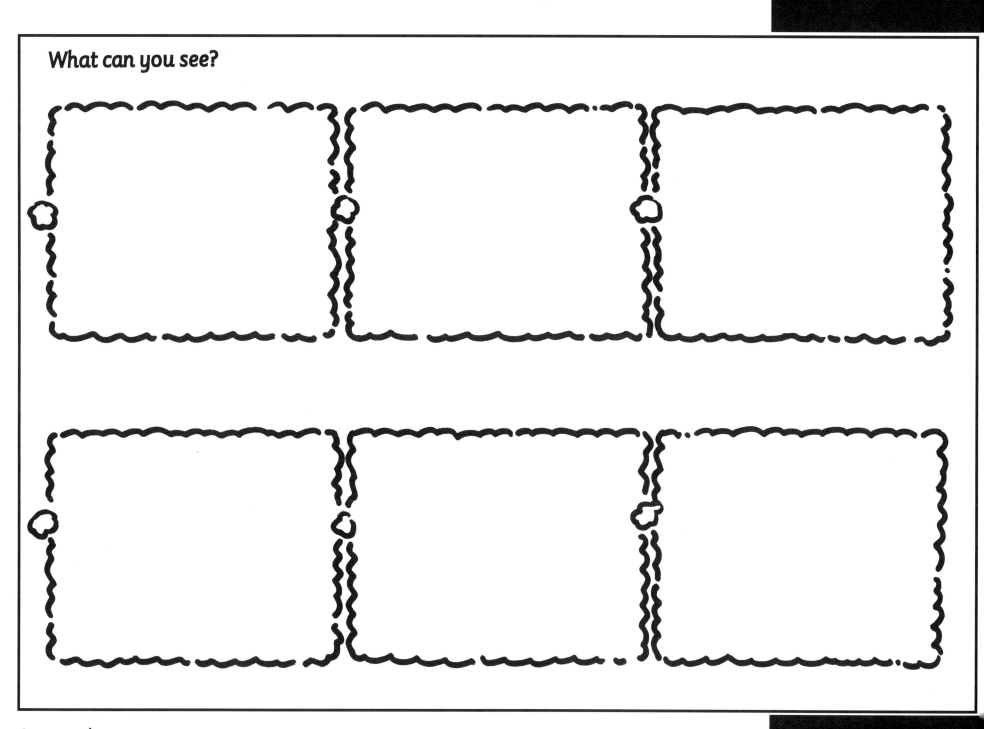

Boiling an egg

● How is an egg boiled? Is there a pattern that must be followed? Perhaps you could watch and remember what happens when somebody boils an egg.

● Ask someone at home to help with the instructions.

● Please bring your pictures or instructions into school.

impact MATHS HOMEWORK

Pairs

YOU WILL NEED: a pack of playing cards.

- Remove the face (picture) cards and all the black cards and use the jokers as 0.

  - Spread out the remaining cards face down.

    - Take turns with someone to pick up two cards.

      - If the total is 10 you may keep the cards. If not, replace them.

        - The winner is the person with the most pairs.

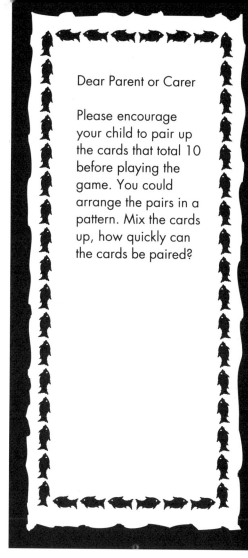

Dear Parent or Carer

Please encourage your child to pair up the cards that total 10 before playing the game. You could arrange the pairs in a pattern. Mix the cards up, how quickly can the cards be paired?

_____and

child

_____

helper(s)

_____

did this activity together

_____and

child

_____

helper(s)

_____

did this activity together

Three cards to make 10

YOU WILL NEED: all the cards from a pack except the face (picture) cards. The joker can have a value of 0.

● Arrange the remaining cards so that you can see the numbers.

● How quickly can you arrange the cards in threes that total 10?

● Perhaps someone could time you to see if you can get faster.

● Can you arrange the cards in a pattern?

impact MATHS HOMEWORK

Ten LEGO pieces

YOU WILL NEED: ten LEGO bricks and some raisins. Take it in turns with someone to play.

● The first player takes away some LEGO pieces while the second player is not looking. The second player turns round and explains what has happened. For example, 'Seven left, so three bricks were taken.' If you are right, take a raisin.

● The second player now has a turn at hiding some LEGO.

● Play the game several times. Are you getting any quicker?

● Which take aways are hard? Which ones are easy? Why?

Dear Parent or Carer

You can play this game using the fingers of both hands. Some fingers can be hidden. Can your child tell you how many are hidden? Please allow your child to have turns at testing you.

_____and

child

_____

helper(s)

_____

did this activity together

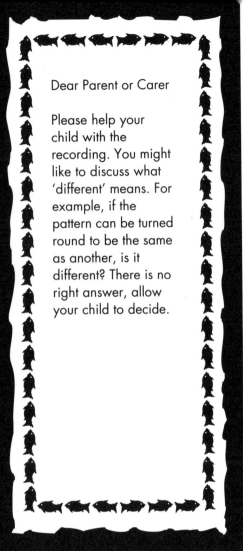
_____and

child

_____

helper(s)

_____

did this activity together

Penny patterns

YOU WILL NEED: *five 1p pieces.*

● Arrange the coins in a pattern and draw round them carefully.

● How many different patterns can you make with the five coins touching?

impact MATHS HOMEWORK

Teachers' Notes
Y E A R   O N E

All these activities provide opportunities for children to use and apply their mathematical skills outside the context of the classroom. This means that every activity will address some aspects of the 'Using and Applying' part of the Programme of Study (was AT1). Commonly children may be expected to do the following whilst sharing IMPACT activity:
● use and apply mathematics in practical tasks and in real-life problems,
● find their own way through tasks, explaining what they do as they go,
● develop their own strategies and discuss these with others, and
● give and follow instructions, and talk about their results.

These are important parts of 'Using and Applying' mathematics. The evidence from OFSTED and other reports now clearly demonstrates that IMPACT can have a marked affect in this area of children's mathematical development.

The activities in this book also address aspects of the Programme of Study for number, specifically in relation to number patterns. In particular, this section utilises the following skills:
● recognising and using simple counting patterns,
● recognising and using simple addition and subtraction patterns, including the use of a 'missing number',
● recognising even and odd numbers, up to 20 and occasionally beyond,
● recognising simple sequences,
● building up square numbers and recognising these, and
● recognising line symmetry.

Square corners Check that the children have found the same pattern. Is it a pattern of odd or even numbers or both? Can they make the pattern symmetrical with Multilink? How many in each layer? Is it still a pattern of odd numbers? The patterns can be reproduced and displayed using squared paper. Questions can be asked such as, 'What will the next three patterns be?' This activity could be displayed in a class book.

Growing squares The children's work can be displayed in a class book. Can they explain how their patterns grew? They could be asked questions such as 'How many small squares are in the fourth large square?' Also, they may like to investigate other growing patterns.

My growing pattern Please give the children an opportunity to share their ideas with a friend. These ideas can be displayed with explanations as to how their patterns continue. The children can predict what might happen next in each of the patterns. Can they design a pattern then that will shrink?

What can it be? The children may like to work in pairs to produce numbers and signs on sheets of paper. These can be arranged to show several sums. The children can take turns to be responsible for turning over a few numbers and trying to work out the answers.

Guess which domino is hiding The children could work in groups to produce different totals using the dominoes. Then they could try to work out what is happening to the dominoes in other groups. One domino pattern could be Blu-tacked on to a surface and each day a different domino placed next to it, with the children set the task of continuing the pattern.

Can you find the missing number? The children can play this game during spare moments. They could produce a pattern demonstrating all the possible arrangements up to 10. This can be recorded on a large sheet of paper and displayed; for example, 10 and 0, 9 and 1 and so on.

Number snake The children could count in threes and shade in the numbers on a hundred number square. Can they see how the pattern repeats itself? Where will the next diagonal line begin? How do they know? They could make a class book with their snakes and number squares. A class picture could be produced where everything is grouped in threes.

Patterns The children enjoy having their patterns used. The designs could be photocopied as worksheets and stuck into a class book to be used as challenges when the children have spare moments. They may like to attempt a pattern that uses negative numbers.

2, 4, 6 pattern The children can extend this activity to 20. They could sit in a circle, each with a 2p or two 1p coins, and count in two as the go round the circle. Can they count backwards in twos? Can they count forwards beginning at 10?

Piles of 2p coins Introduce the children to odd and even numbers. Share the patterns that they have brought to school. These could be recorded on a large number line using different colours for odd and even numbers. The children may like to arrange squares in pairs and pairs with odd ones by the numbers to show odd and even numbers.

What can the question be? Have any of the children found a pattern in their answers? They could sit in groups and use apparatus to record additional patterns using two numbers. What about take away patterns? A large number 10 could be displayed and the children's ideas put

round the edge. New ideas could be added as they are discovered.

Oh dear! Record all the children's ideas in a class book and discuss different ways of solving the same problem. Investigate how many different methods can be produced for one calculation. The children could write their methods on paper. Can they be arranged to show a pattern?

Chocolate bar machine The children may like to extend this activity. Groups could sell their chocolate bar at different prices. The different ways of buying these chocolate bars could be recorded and displayed in a class book with illustrations of their chocolate bars.

It may be advisable to limit the cost of a bar to 50p or limit the number of coins permissible.

Vending machine The children may like to bring empty soft drink cans to school and set up a shop. They could price the cans, but the customers must use 50p coins for buying. Change should be limited to 5p and 10p coins (this has implications for the pricing). Other challenges could be set to allow for differentiation.

Design a spiral pattern The children could investigate other patterns, for example, using odd numbers, even numbers or a shorter number sequence. Their ideas, together with those produced at home, could be displayed and questions asked, such as, 'How was this pattern produced? Can you find a pattern that was produced using odd numbers?' and so on.

Odd and even The children can play this game in class, writing down *all* their throws – not just the ones they score. They will need to make two columns. How much do the 'unsuccessful' throws add up to. Who is likely to get the highest score, the person who is 'odd' or the person who is 'even'? Make a large dice with the numbers coloured according to whether they are odd or even. Extend this to a number line.

Match this number The children can collate their information and make a graph of the number of throws they each had to have. What was the fewest number? What was the most? Was it easier to leave the odd numbers or to leave the even numbers? Reinforce their knowledge of even and odd numbers by counting in even and in odd numbers.

Even coins The children can compare their amounts. Did everyone include *all* the coins? What about notes? Consider £5 notes, £10 notes and so on. Suppose all the 'odd' coins were to be removed, which amounts would be most difficult to make?

Ready, steady, go! The children can play again in class, only this time writing down all the sums they do; for example, 2 + 4 + 5 + 1 = 12 (where the fingers turned down are represented by those numbers). What totals do they get? Do even or odd numbers occur more frequently? Make a class graph of all the totals.

Noisy dice The children can play a similar game in class; throwing the dice and writing the numbers in the correct columns – an 'even' column or an 'odd' column. If they throw the dice twenty times, which column adds up to the most? Does it always work like this? Why?

Domestic evens The children can display the items they have collected in sets according to their numbers. What examples of 2, 4, or 6 did they find? What were the highest and lowest even numbers they found? Can they make a similar list of examples of odd numbers around the school?

Sixes galore The children can write out the 'story' of other numbers, such as 5 or 7, as well as that of 6. Thus, the story of 4 goes: 1 + 1 + 1 + 1 = 4, 1 + 3 = 4, 2 + 2 = 4. The 'story' of 8 or 9 is really long! How can the children be sure they have found all the combinations? Look at the patterns which emerge if you lay one 'story' beside another.

Nine, nine, nine! Can the children demonstrate that they have found all the nines? Can they use the same principle to find all the ways of making ten? Which of the ways of making ten can be done using coins? (For example, there is no 3p coin!)

LEGO sums The children can draw some LEGO sums using a 'plate' as one of the piles. Can they create them sensibly? For example, do they sometimes produce sums like this: 7 + ● = 3, which might indicate that they do not understand how these sums work. Some children may be able to create sums using subtraction 10 – ● = 7.

Ladder sums The children can exchange their ladder sums and try doing each others. Bring in some spare ones for those who did not make up any at home. Make a class book of ladder sums. Have some with two figures missing. How many possible 'answers' are there to these ladders?

Letter sums The children can exchange their letter sums and try doing each others. Bring some spare ones for those who did not make up any at home. Make a class book of letter sums or display them in sets according to the solution (that is, all those with a solution of 4 go in one set and so on).

How many possible 'answers' are there to the letter sums with several letters?

Card turn-ups The children can play the same game on paper in class, but writing down the pairs they make by putting their cards side by side. Tell them to write the numbers in two columns – one headed 'even' and one headed 'odd'.

Even and odd names The children can collate their information either in groups or as a whole class. all the names can be put into two sets – even and odd. Make a long list of even numbers and a long list of odd numbers. Discuss how we can tell if a number is even or odd just by looking at it.

Book pages The children can collate their numbers into two giant lists, placing the numbers in order of size. This will raise questions of place value (recognising the size of the different numbers). It will also provoke a discussion as to how they know whether the numbers are even or odd.

Folding a square The children can investigate how they folded their squares. What shapes and patterns did they produce? Were there squares, triangles or rectangles? Does the type of folding affect the result? Can anyone explain what has happened? How soon do the numbers get larger than 100?

Counting in tens This is an excellent game for helping children to understand the significance of the first digit. They could sit in a circle and each take two numbers and make the smaller number. Everyone then moves to sit in number order. Can they use 10p and 1p coins to show their answers? Then everyone can make their numbers ten larger or ten smaller. Ask them to read out their new numbers, are they still in the same order? Why?

Times table game The children could stick their activities into a class book and/ or a large wall picture could be made to reproduce the grid. The children could continue to practise their multiplication skills using the card and coin method and refer to the chart for checking.

Tens are special This activity can be extended in class to adding and taking away 11p. Can the children write the pattern? Decimetre strips could be used to demonstrate the pattern. These could be displayed and questions could be asked, such as 'How many decimetres in 43?' or 'Three decimetres plus three centimetres equals what?'

Teen numbers Use Dienes' blocks and several cards marked 1 and others number 0-9 with small groups of children. Let them each take a 1 and any other number. Which teen numbers can they make? Can they sit in number order? Who has the biggest number? What happens if you take the 'ten card' away?

Along and up The children may like to draw a large map of an imaginary playground or park or of their local area. This can be divided into squares and small models made to place in the squares. What are the models' locations? Can the children move the models to newly specified locations?

Design your own map The children may like to draw large versions of their favourite map designs. Number the squares clearly. Add questions; for example, 'In which square is the swing? Who can move the swing to square (2, 4)?'

impact MATHS HOMEWORK

Square corners

- Carry on colouring the corner of the grid.

- Record the numbers of squares coloured each time.

- Can you see what is happening to the numbers?

- Can you predict what will happen next?

- Can you explain to someone what you have noticed?

yellow	yellow	yellow						
blue	blue	yellow						
red	blue	yellow						

Dear Parent or Carer

Please help your child to record the number of squares coloured each time. Ask your child the questions and give time for a reply.

_____and

child

_____

helper(s)

_____

did this activity together

_____and

child

_____

helper(s)

_____

did this activity together

Growing squares

● Keep colouring each 'picture frame' using a different colour.

			blue	blue	blue		
			blue	red	blue		
			blue	blue	blue		

impact MATHS HOMEWORK

Growing squares

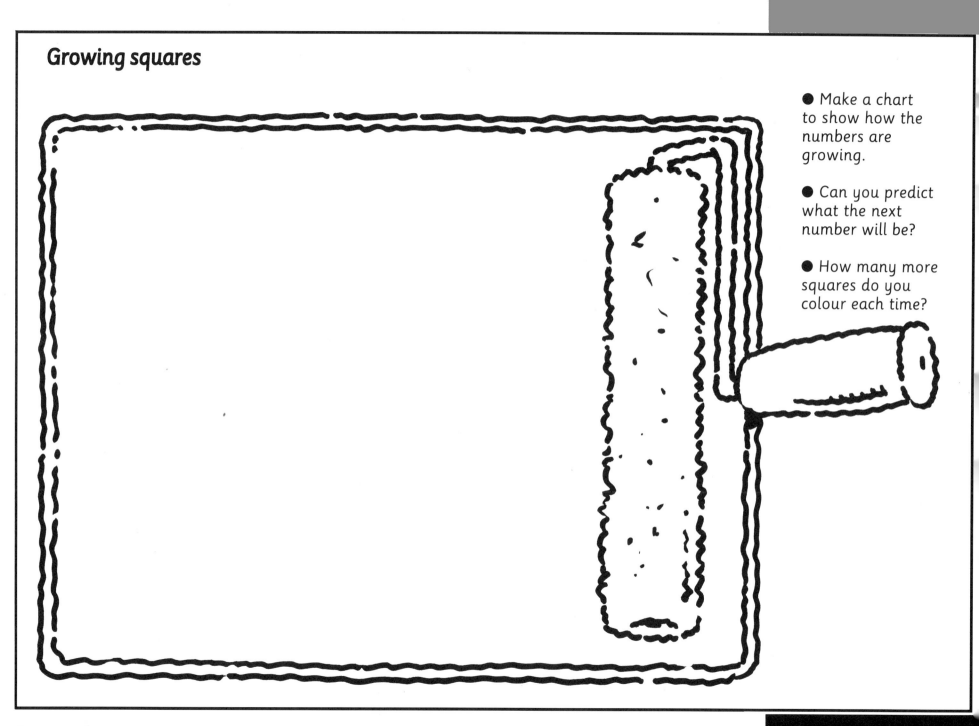

● Make a chart to show how the numbers are growing.

● Can you predict what the next number will be?

● How many more squares do you colour each time?

_____and

child

_____

helper(s)

_____

did this activity together

My growing pattern

		blue							
	blue		blue						
red	blue	red	blue	red					
	blue		blue						
			blue						

● Can you continue this growing pattern?

● What is happening to the design?

● Can you predict what comes next?

● Record the numbers as you colour your pattern.

impact MATHS HOMEWORK

What can it be?

YOU WILL NEED: a set of cards numbered 1–10 and the sign cards on this sheet.

● Please cut out the sign cards and use them to make a sum; for example, 6 + 4 = 10.

● Now play this game with a partner.

• The first player makes a sum and then turns over one of the cards in the sum. The second player must not see anything that is happening until the first person has turned over the card.
• The second player turns round and tries to guess (work out) which card has been turned over and explains why.
• Take turns and keep a score.

● Can you play this game if two cards are turned over?

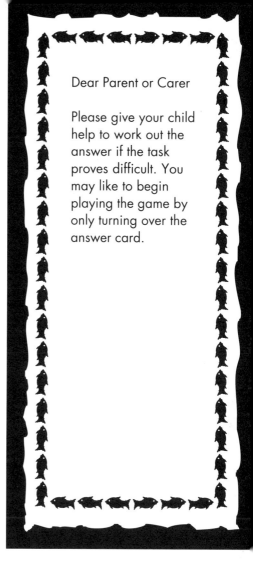

Dear Parent or Carer

Please give your child help to work out the answer if the task proves difficult. You may like to begin playing the game by only turning over the answer card.

_____and

child

_____

helper(s)

_____

did this activity together

_____and

child

_____

helper(s)

_____

did this activity together

Guess which domino is hiding

YOU WILL NEED: a set of dominoes.

● Lay out the dominoes in a pattern.
(In the example at the bottom of the
page the totals are 6.) Continue until
you have used all of the dominoes.

● Now play a game with a partner.

• The first player must turn around and
not look while the second player turns
over one domino.
• The first player turns back and tries
to work out which numbers are on the
missing domino.
• Take turns.

● Arrange the dominoes in another
pattern and take turns again.

impact MATHS HOMEWORK

Can you find the missing number?

YOU WILL NEED: all the numbered cards in a pack – use the jokers as 0. The face (picture) cards must be taken out.

● The idea is to find the difference between the card you have been dealt and ten.

● Play the game with a partner to help you remember your number bonds.

● Your partner deals a card and you must find the difference between the card and ten.

● Take turns. Are some differences easier than others?

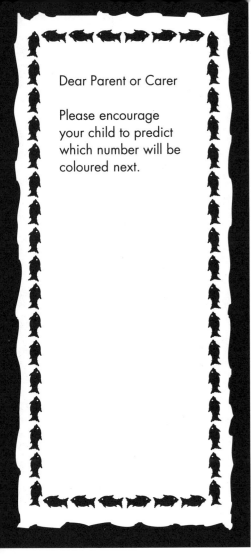
Number snake

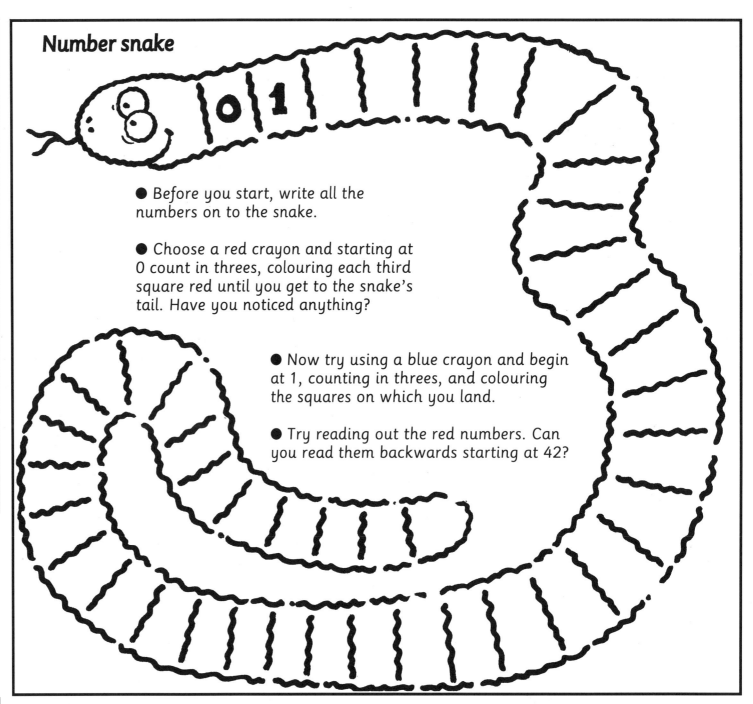

● Before you start, write all the numbers on to the snake.

● Choose a red crayon and starting at 0 count in threes, colouring each third square red until you get to the snake's tail. Have you noticed anything?

● Now try using a blue crayon and begin at 1, counting in threes, and colouring the squares on which you land.

● Try reading out the red numbers. Can you read them backwards starting at 42?

impact MATHS HOMEWORK

Patterns

● Can you work out what is happening in this pattern?

● Write down in the triangles the differences between the numbers.

● Can you carry on the pattern?

● What about this pattern:

● Please design a pattern for your friend to try in school next week.

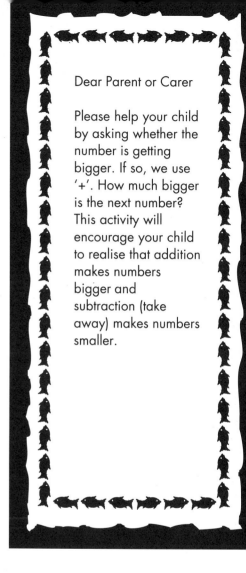
_____and

child

_____

helper(s)

_____

did this activity together

impact MATHS HOMEWORK

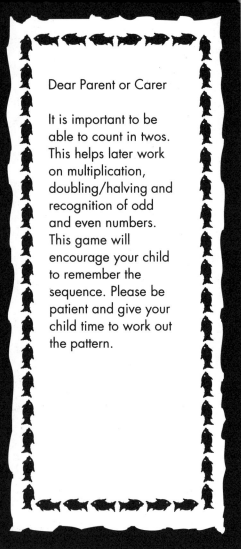
2, 4, 6 pattern

YOU WILL NEED: the red cards (hearts and diamonds) numbered 1–10 from a pack.

● Shuffle the cards and arrange them face down on the table.

● The first player should turn over two cards. You are looking for a 2.

● If you have a 2, keep it to begin your pattern. Remember the numbers on the cards that you have to replace, you may need them later.

● Then the second player picks up two cards and tries to begin their pattern.

● Take turns. Once you have found a 2 you will need to look out for a 4.

● The first player to get to 10, by collecting the cards in order, 2, 4, 6, 8 and 10, is the winner.

● The same game can be played beginning at 10 and going back in twos. You could use the jokers to represent 0.

impact MATHS HOMEWORK

Piles of 2p coins

YOU WILL NEED: the 1–10 cards from one suit of a pack of playing cards and lots of 2p pieces.

● Turn the cards upside down.

● Take a card and look at the number.

● Now take that number of 2p coins and try to build two equal towers.

● Were you able to do this? If so, it is an even number of coins. If not, it is an odd number.

● Record the card numbers and say whether your towers were odd or even.

● Write the card numbers in order. What do you notice? Is there a pattern?

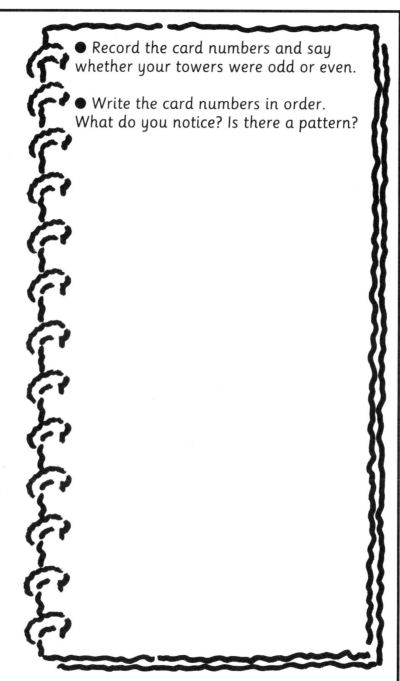

Dear Parent or Carer

Please help your child to record the results and to look for patterns in the results.

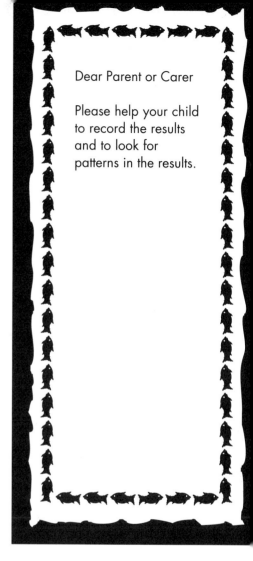

_____and
child

_____
helper(s)

_____

did this activity together

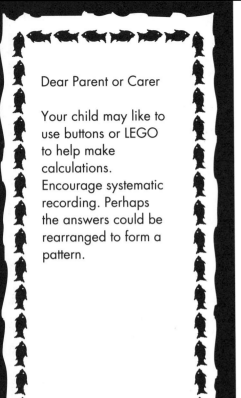

_____and

child

_____

helper(s)

_____

did this activity together

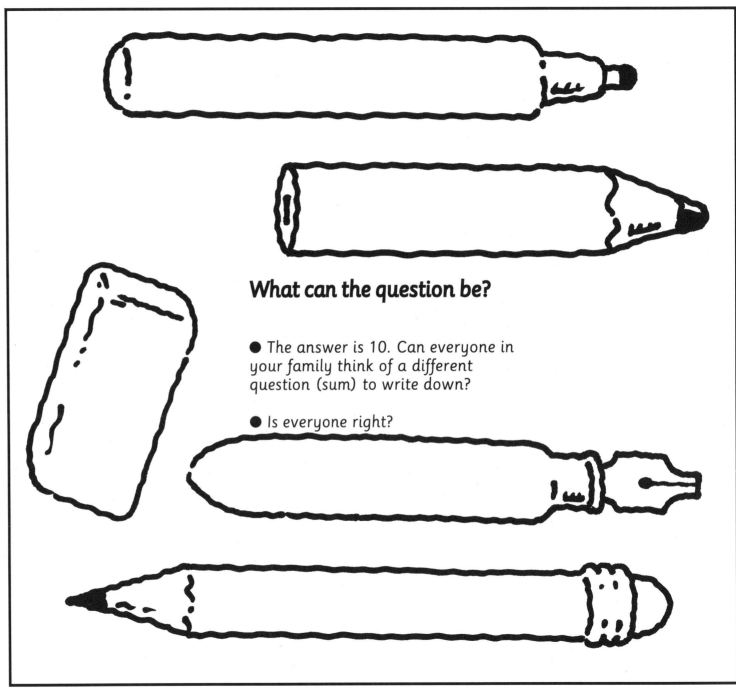

What can the question be?

● The answer is 10. Can everyone in your family think of a different question (sum) to write down?

● Is everyone right?

impact MATHS HOMEWORK

Oh dear!

● The number 5 is broken on my calculator and I have some sums to do:

$5 + 4$ $5 - 3$ $5 + 5$ $8 - 5$

● Can you make these calculations on the calculator using other numbers instead of 5?

● Write down your new calculations and bring them to school.

Dear Parent or Carer

There are many ways in which each calculation can be answered. Please give your child time to investigate their ideas. Your child may like to use buttons or LEGO to help with alternative calculations.

_____and

child

_____

helper(s)

_____

did this activity together

Chocolate bar machine

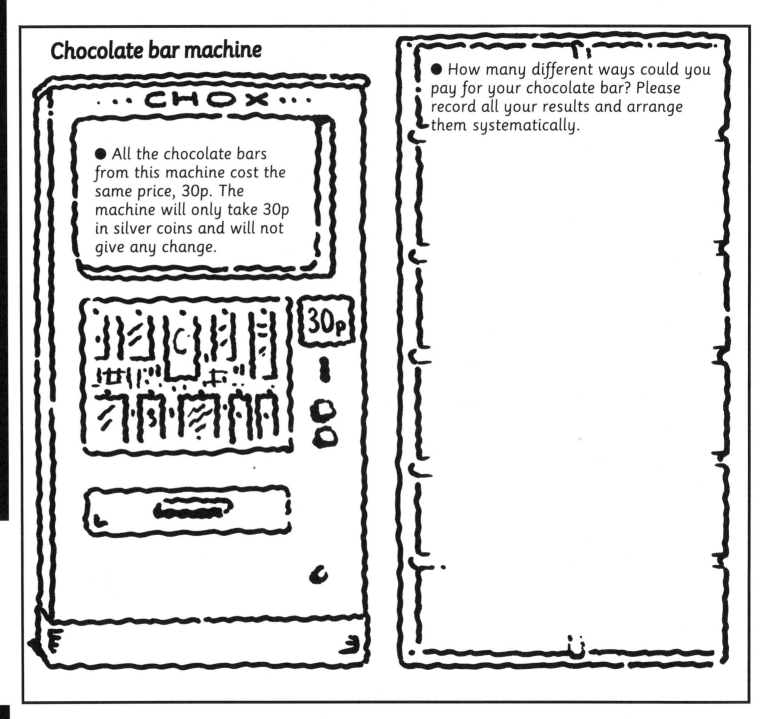

● All the chocolate bars from this machine cost the same price, 30p. The machine will only take 30p in silver coins and will not give any change.

● How many different ways could you pay for your chocolate bar? Please record all your results and arrange them systematically.

impact MATHS HOMEWORK

Vending machine

● This vending machine will only take 50p coins. Drinks cost 35p. How much change will the machine give you back?

● The machine is only able to return 5p and 10p coins. Can you think of the different ways that you can have your change?

● Can you arrange your answers in an order?

● How do you know when you have found all the arrangements?

● Make a list of the final order and bring into school.

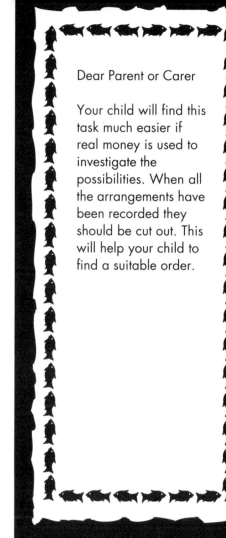

Dear Parent or Carer

Your child will find this task much easier if real money is used to investigate the possibilities. When all the arrangements have been recorded they should be cut out. This will help your child to find a suitable order.

_____and

child

_____

helper(s)

_____

did this activity together

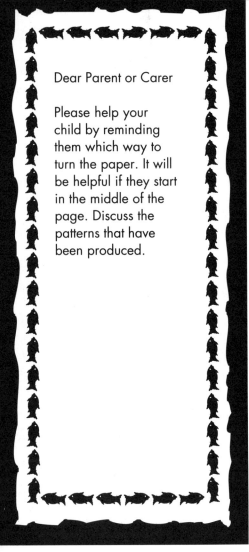
Design a spiral pattern

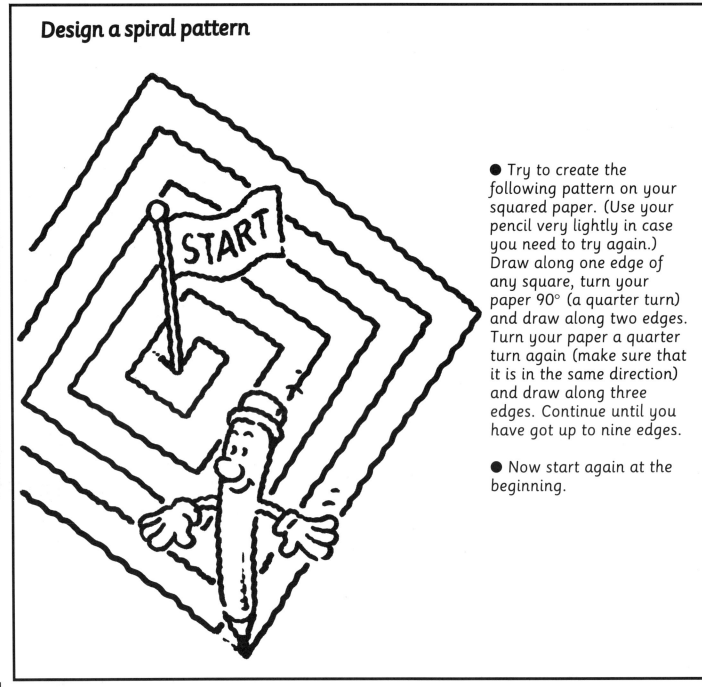

● Try to create the following pattern on your squared paper. (Use your pencil very lightly in case you need to try again.) Draw along one edge of any square, turn your paper 90° (a quarter turn) and draw along two edges. Turn your paper a quarter turn again (make sure that it is in the same direction) and draw along three edges. Continue until you have got up to nine edges.

● Now start again at the beginning.

impact MATHS HOMEWORK

Design a spiral pattern

_____and

child

_____

helper(s)

_____

did this activity together

Odd and even

YOU WILL NEED: a dice, a paper and pencil for scoring and a pile of counters (small bricks or dried pasta will do).

● Decide in advance who is going to be 'even' and who is going to be 'odd'!

● Take it in turns to throw the dice.

● If you throw an even number and you are 'even', score that number – that is, write it down. Use the space opposite.

● If you throw an odd number and you are 'odd', score that number. If you throw the wrong type of number, take a counter.

● Keep taking it in turns and throwing the dice until someone has collected six counters.

● Add up all your scores. The person with the score nearest to 18 wins.

impact MATHS HOMEWORK

Match the number

YOU WILL NEED: a dice and a pile of used matches (small bricks or counters will do instead).

● Make a number line of used matches from 1 to 12. Arrange them in piles.

● Throw the dice either ONCE or TWICE. If twice, add the totals; for example, 2 + 6 = 8. Write down what you get in one of the spaces below. If it is an even number, remove the matches from the appropriate number on the line. In the example, I would remove the 8 matches.

● How many throws did you need before you had removed all the even numbers leaving a number line with just the odd numbers?

● Play again, but this time only remove the odd numbered piles of matches. Use the second set of spaces to write down all your throws. How many throws did you have this time?

● Bring all your work into school.

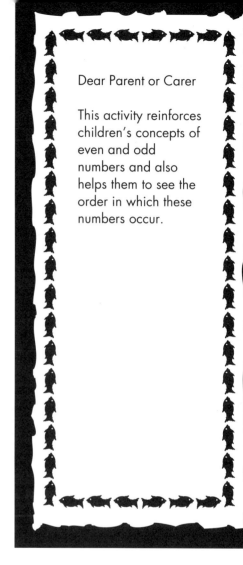

Dear Parent or Carer

This activity reinforces children's concepts of even and odd numbers and also helps them to see the order in which these numbers occur.

_____and

child

_____

helper(s)

_____

did this activity together

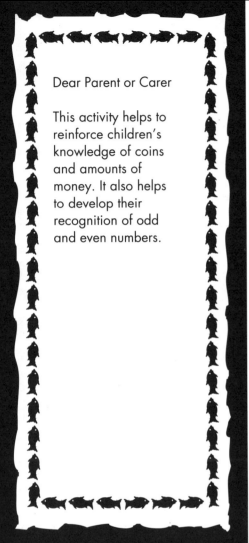

_____and

child

_____

helper(s)

_____

did this activity together

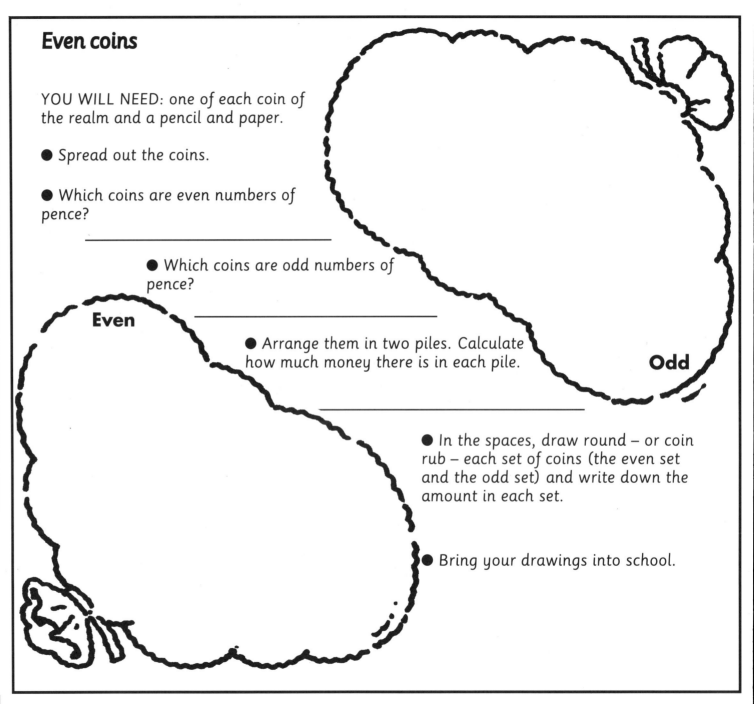

Even coins

YOU WILL NEED: one of each coin of the realm and a pencil and paper.

● Spread out the coins.

● Which coins are even numbers of pence?

_____

● Which coins are odd numbers of pence?

Even

_____

● Arrange them in two piles. Calculate how much money there is in each pile.

Odd

_____

● In the spaces, draw round – or coin rub – each set of coins (the even set and the odd set) and write down the amount in each set.

● Bring your drawings into school.

impact MATHS HOMEWORK

Ready, steady, go!

● First decide who is going to be 'evens' and who is going to be 'odds'.

● Both of you put your hands behind your backs.

● You say, 'Ready, steady, go!' and you both bring your hands out from behind your backs with some of the fingers turned down.

● Count the total number of fingers which are folded down on all four hands.

● If the total is even, the 'even' person scores that number. If the total number folded down is odd, the 'odd' person scores that total. Write your scores on the hand shapes below.

● Play until one person's score reaches 25 or over. He or she wins.

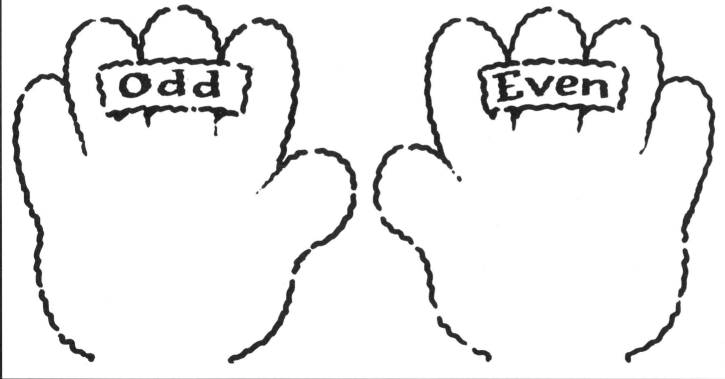

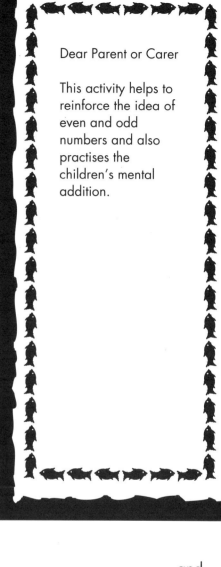

Dear Parent or Carer

This activity helps to reinforce the idea of even and odd numbers and also practises the children's mental addition.

_____and

child

_____

helper(s)

_____

did this activity together

Noisy dice

YOU WILL NEED: a dice and a large pile of small counters, such as dried pasta or bricks.

● Take it in turns to throw the dice. Before you throw it, say whether you are going to get an odd number or an even number.

● If you are right, take that number of counters.

● If you are wrong, make that number of animal noises – choose an animal to be first!

● The first person to collect 18 counters is the winner.

MOO!

impact MATHS HOMEWORK

Domestic evens

● Look around your home. How many examples of even numbers can you find?

● Are there an even number of people in your home?

● Are there an even number of doors? Of stairs? Of windows?

● Collect as many examples of even numbers as you can and write them in the space provided.

● Bring your lists into school.

Number	Example

Dear Parent or Carer

We are working on odd and even numbers. This work helps the children to reinforce these ideas.

_____and
child

_____
helper(s)

_____
did this activity together

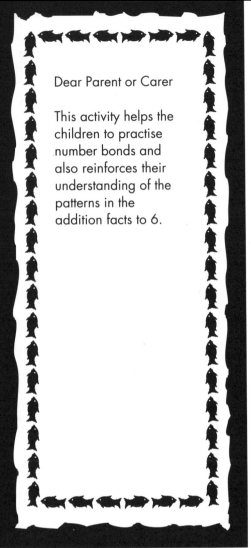

Sixes galore

YOU WILL NEED: a pencil and a dice.

● Choose four sets of balloons each.

● Write numbers in each of your balloons BUT each set must add up to six.

Thus, one set might be 1 + 3 + 2, another might be 3 + 3 and so on. All the sets must be different.

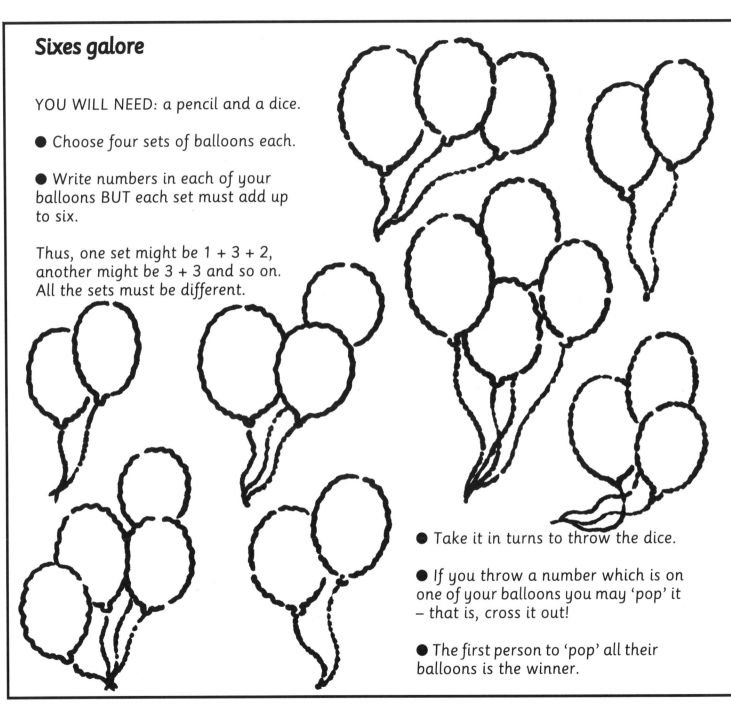

● Take it in turns to throw the dice.

● If you throw a number which is on one of your balloons you may 'pop' it – that is, cross it out!

● The first person to 'pop' all their balloons is the winner.

impact MATHS HOMEWORK

Nine, nine, nine!

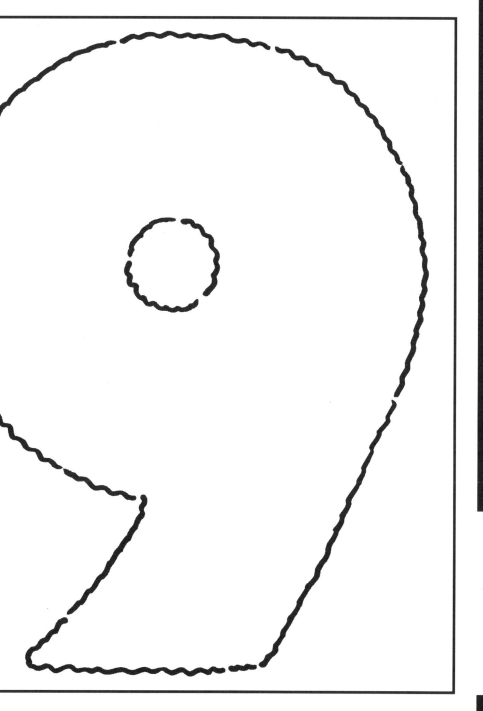

● How many different ways are there of making 9?

● Between 9 + 0 and 1 + 1 + 1 + 1 + 1 + 1 + 1 + 1 + 1, how many completely different ways of making 9 can you find?

PS We only want ones which involve adding up!

PPS How can you show that you have found them all?!

● Record all your ways of making 9 on this sheet and bring them into school.

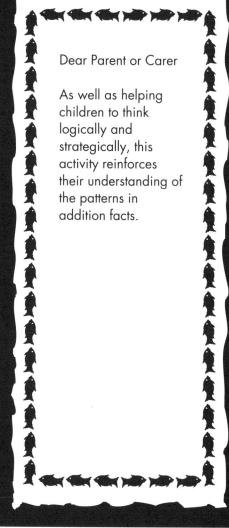

Dear Parent or Carer

As well as helping children to think logically and strategically, this activity reinforces their understanding of the patterns in addition facts.

_____and

child

_____

helper(s)

_____

did this activity together

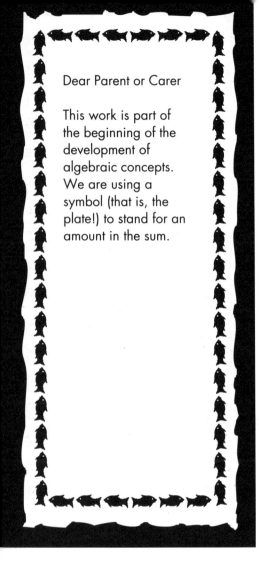
LEGO sums

YOU WILL NEED: some LEGO bricks (or counters or dried pasta), a plate, some paper and a pencil. You will need to make a '+' sign and an '=' sign out of paper.

● Ask your helper to turn round or shut their eyes. Lay out a LEGO sum.

For example, 4 + 6 = 10

● Put a piece of paper or a plate over one of the amounts in the sum:

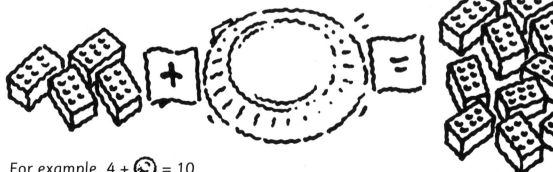

For example, 4 + 😊 = 10

● The helper has to tell you how many are in the covered-up pile.

● Now your helper can lay out a sum and cover one of the amounts. Can you work out what it is?

● Have three goes each.

impact MATHS HOMEWORK

Ladder sums

● Look at the first ladder below. The numbers on the rungs add up to the number on the top!

● The ladder next to it has a number missing. Talk to someone about what number you think is missing.

● Write it in.

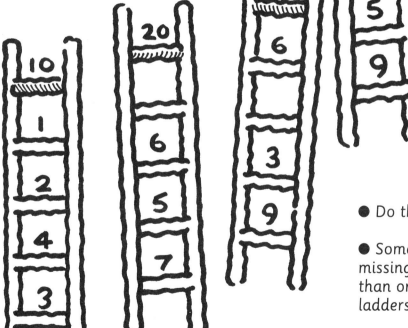

● Do the same with the other ladders.

● Some of them have more than one missing number. Could there be more than one right answer for those ladders?

● Make up your own ladder sum for someone else at school to do.

● Bring all your work into school.

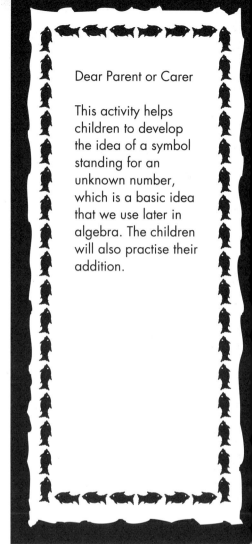

_____and

child

_____

helper(s)

_____

did this activity together

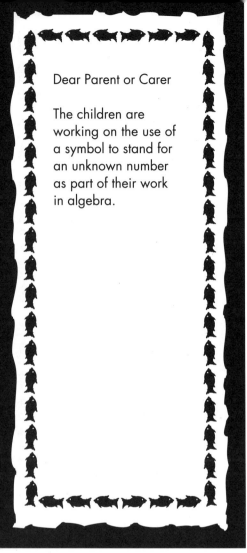
Letter sums

● Ask someone to help you to make up some letter sums. They look like this:

13 + R = 32

● You can use which ever letters you like!

● Try making up some which have more than one letter.

● Work out the solutions to all the sums you make up and write them on the back of this piece of paper. Remember that there may be more than one solution to the sums with more than one letter in them!

impact MATHS HOMEWORK

Card turn-ups

YOU WILL NEED: a pack of playing cards with the face (picture) cards and the tens removed.

● Decide who is going to be 'evens' and who is going to be 'odds'.

● Deal out a pair of cards to each player, face down in front of them.

● Each person must look at their cards and put them side by side to try to make an even two-digit number if they are 'evens' or an odd two-digit number if they are 'odds'.

● Each person who succeeds keeps their pair of cards.

● If they cannot succeed, that pair of cards is put on the bottom of the pile.

● Two more cards are dealt to each player.

● Keep playing until one person has ten pairs.

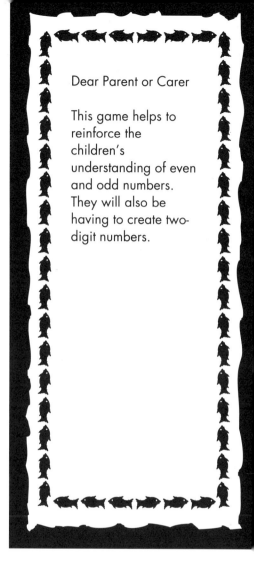

Dear Parent or Carer

This game helps to reinforce the children's understanding of even and odd numbers. They will also be having to create two-digit numbers.

_____and

child

_____

helper(s)

_____

did this activity together

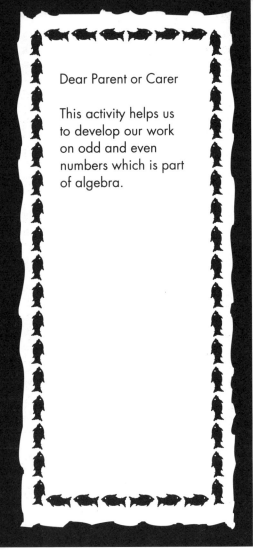
Even and odd names

● Find as many friends and relations as you can and ask them to write down their first names.

● Count how many letters each name has and then write it into one of the two sets below.

● How many names can you put in each set?

odd

even

● Draw a picture below of one of the people you asked and bring all your work into school.

impact MATHS HOMEWORK

Book pages

● Choose a book. Are there an even or an odd number of pages in your book?

● Ask someone to help you. Write down the number of pages in your book. If it is even, write it in red. If it is odd, write it in blue.

● Find another book. Are there an even or an odd number of pages in that one? Write down the number in the right colour.

● Find the longest book in your home! How many pages does it have? Write down the number in the right colour.

_____and

child

_____

helper(s)

_____

did this activity together

Folding a square

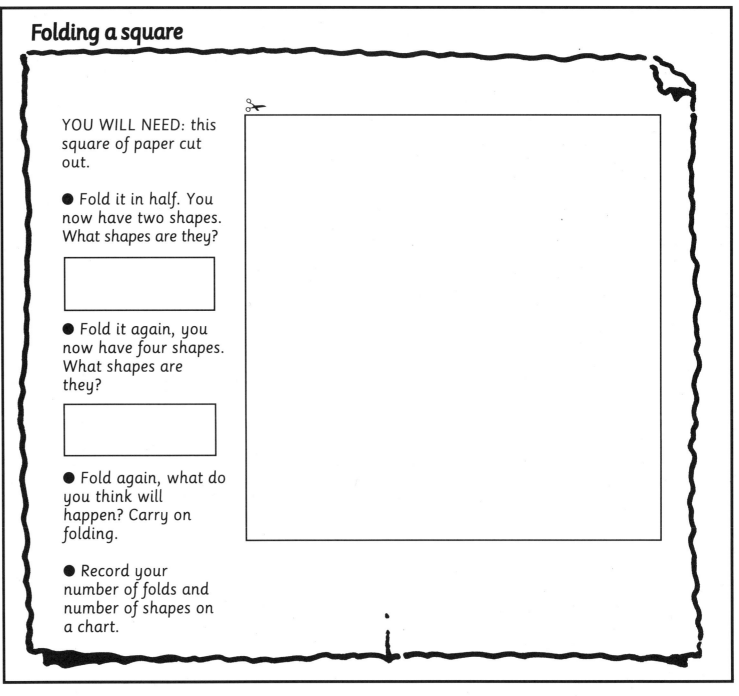

YOU WILL NEED: this square of paper cut out.

● Fold it in half. You now have two shapes. What shapes are they?

● Fold it again, you now have four shapes. What shapes are they?

● Fold again, what do you think will happen? Carry on folding.

● Record your number of folds and number of shapes on a chart.

impact MATHS HOMEWORK

Counting in tens

YOU WILL NEED: several 10p coins, many 1p coins and some currants or raisins.

● Cut out the cards below and place them in two piles face down.

● Take turns to play this game.

● Take a card from each pile and make a number; for example ☐3 ☐6. Make the number with 10p and 1p coins; for example, 3 tens and 6 ones (units).

● Make the number 10p more. What is your new number? Check on your calculator to see if you are right.

● Replace the coins and cards and collect a raisin if you were right.

● Play several times, the winner is the one who has the most raisins. Enjoy eating the raisins!

0	1	2
3	4	5

6	7	0	1	2	3	4
8	9	5	6	7	8	9

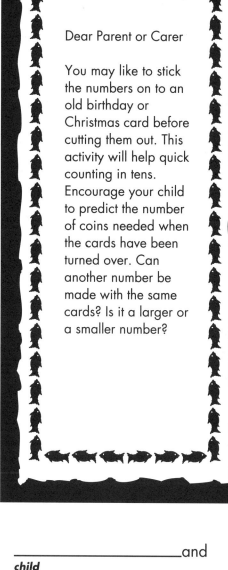

Dear Parent or Carer

You may like to stick the numbers on to an old birthday or Christmas card before cutting them out. This activity will help quick counting in tens. Encourage your child to predict the number of coins needed when the cards have been turned over. Can another number be made with the same cards? Is it a larger or a smaller number?

_____and

child

_____

helper(s)

_____

did this activity together

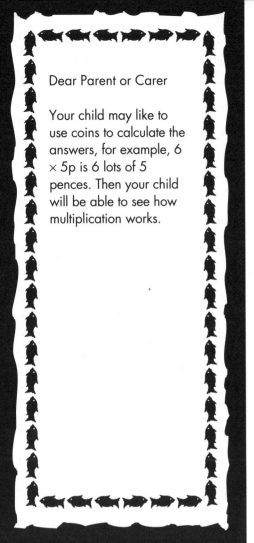

_____and

child

_____

helper(s)

_____

did this activity together

Times table game

YOU WILL NEED: 2p, 5p and 10p coins, all the red 1–10 playing cards from a pack, three coloured pencils (a red one for 2p, a blue one for 5p and a yellow one for 10p) and the hundred square opposite. A calculator will be useful for checking.

● Place the playing cards face down in a pile.

● Play this game with a partner.

● Take a card from the pile and a coin. Multiply them together. For example, 6 multiplied by 5p.

● Check your answer on the calculator. If you are right, colour the square showing the answer in the hundred square with the right coloured crayon (blue for this example).

● Replace the coin and the card at the bottom of the pile.

● Take turns to repeat the game.

1	2	3	4	5	6	7	8	9	10
11	12	13	14	15	16	17	18	19	20
21	22	23	24	25	26	27	28	29	30
31	32	33	34	35	36	37	38	39	40
41	42	43	44	45	46	47	48	49	50
51	52	53	54	55	56	57	58	59	60
61	62	63	64	65	66	67	68	69	70
71	72	73	74	75	76	77	78	79	80
81	82	83	84	85	86	87	88	89	90
91	92	93	94	95	96	97	98	99	100

● When the numbers in the hundred square have all been coloured, can you see a pattern in each colour? Read out each different-coloured pattern.

● Are there some squares that have more than one colour? Why?

Tens are special

YOU WILL NEED: several 10p coins and a few 1p and 2p coins.

● Make a teens number. For example: 10p, 2p and 1p = 13p.

● Add 10p coins, one at a time, and write all the numbers you make opposite.

● Take the 10p coins away one at a time. Can you see what has happened to your numbers?

● Can you explain the pattern?

● Try another number. For example:
10p, 2p, 2p, 2p, and 1p = 17p

● Can you predict what the numbers will be when you add the 10p coins?

● Write the answers down and check by counting the coins.

Dear Parent or Carer

The pattern of counting in tens is very important when calculating. It will help your child to calculate quickly.

_____and

child

_____

helper(s)

_____

did this activity together

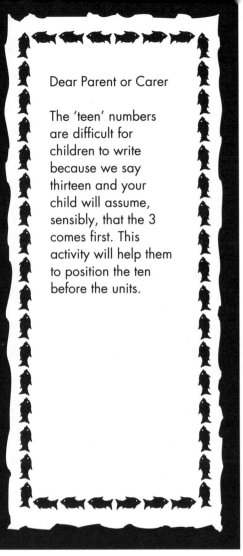

_____and

child

_____

helper(s)

_____

did this activity together

Teen numbers

YOU WILL NEED: a 10p coin and several 1p and 2p coins.

● Use the 1p and 2p coins to make a number, such as 3p.

● Put a 10p in front of the number, what do you have now?

● Take the 3p away, what do you have now?

● Replace the 3p. Predict what will happen when the 10p is removed.

● How quickly can you get the right answer?

● Can you write all the numbers that you make in order?

Along and up

To say where something is on a map like this, always look ALONG the grid first and then UP (along the corridor and up the stairs).

● What is drawn in square (1,2)?

● Can you write the numbers for the squares with the flowers and the treasure chest in?

● Can you draw a pirate in square (6,3)?

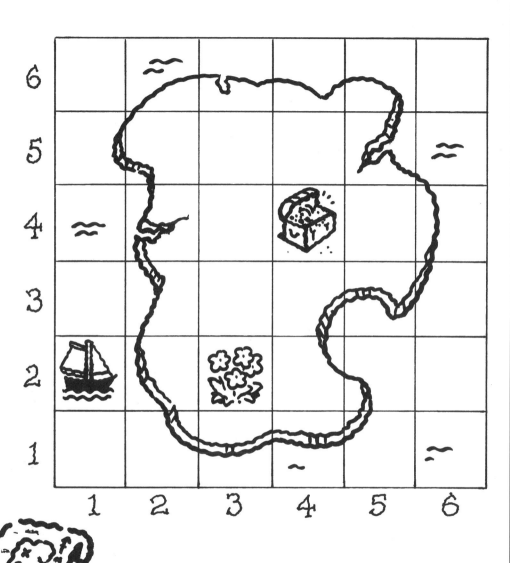

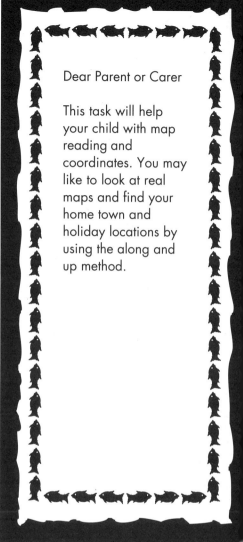

Dear Parent or Carer

This task will help your child with map reading and coordinates. You may like to look at real maps and find your home town and holiday locations by using the along and up method.

_____and

child

_____

helper(s)

_____

did this activity together

Design your own map

```
6 |     |     |     |     |     |     |
  |_____|_____|_____|_____|_____|_____|
5 |     |     |     |     |     |     |
  |_____|_____|_____|_____|_____|_____|
4 |     |     |     |     |     |     |
  |_____|_____|_____|_____|_____|_____|
3 |     |     |     |     |     |     |
  |_____|_____|_____|_____|_____|_____|
2 |     |     |     |     |     |     |
  |_____|_____|_____|_____|_____|_____|
1 |     |     |     |     |     |     |
  |_____|_____|_____|_____|_____|_____|
     1     2     3     4     5     6
```

● Can you draw a map in this grid? It could be an island, your garden or a walk that you enjoy. Put a few special things on to your map in some of the squares. They could be surprises or real things.

● Can you write some questions about your map to ask your friends?

Remember that squares are numbered by going ALONG first and then UP (along the corridor and up the stairs).

impact MATHS HOMEWORK

Teachers' Notes
YEAR TWO

All these activities provide opportunities for children to use and apply their mathematical skills outside the context of the classroom. This means that every activity will address some aspects of the 'Using and Applying' part of the Programme of Study (was AT1). Commonly children may be expected to do the following whilst sharing IMPACT activity:

- use and apply mathematics in practical tasks and in real-life problems,
- find their own way through tasks, explaining what they do as they go,
- develop their own strategies and discuss these with others, and
- give and follow instructions, and talk about their results.

These are important parts of 'Using and Applying' mathematics. The evidence from OFSTED and other reports now clearly demonstrates that IMPACT can have a marked affect in this area of children's mathematical development.

The activities in this book also address aspects of the Programme of Study for number, specifically in relation to number patterns. In particular, this section utilises the following skills:

- using simple function machines,
- constructing and recognising repetitive patterns, including many counting patterns,
- recognising and constructing addition and subtraction patterns, including the use of a 'missing number',
- recognising the even and odd numbers,

- constructing and recognising sequences,
- exploring the patterns on a 0 – 99 grid, and
- beginning to recognise that addition is the inverse of subtraction and vice versa.

The magic rocket Please allow the children to construct a large rocket for display. They can write numbers on to cards as problems for others to solve and will generate lots of class discussion. Alternatively, their rocket ideas can be photocopied and used as class activities.

Coming down to Earth The children may like to design some input and output 'robots', and think of some tasks they might perform. Their own designs could be tried, photocopied and the ideas shared. These can then be displayed near a robot in a class book to give ideas.

Moon landing These operations are often difficult for children to grasp. Six children, in two groups of three, could be used to demonstrate: three standing and three standing equals six. Six standing and then three move away equals three. Write this as 3 + 3 = 6, then 6 – 3 = 3. The children can draw out their own subtraction and addition sums, using the right symbols. The completed rocket activities can be displayed around large model rockets.

Cakes Please give the children time to demonstrate how they solved the problem. How many different ways are there? How can they record their work? They could work in groups to solve different problems using the same number of cubes. Ask the children to find out how many ways the cubes (cakes) can be packed.

Halving The children can order their strips by length and explain how they solved this problem. Some may like to demonstrate their ideas. This could lead to an investigation of finding half a carrot, half a beaker of sand, half a square or half their age and so on. This could make a very attractive display to demonstrate halving.

Halving numbers Let the children explain their findings. They may like to do this by colouring a large number square. Which numbers halve several times? Which numbers will not halve once exactly?

Calculator challenge Please make sure that the children are familiar with addition and subtraction before they try this activity. Give them time to explain how they used their calculators to confirm their answers. They may like to demonstrate the activity with cubes, for example: 3 x 5 = 15, 15 ? 5 = 3. Can they try 5 x 3 = 15? They could make pictures to illustrate this.

Calculator operations The children may like to use apparatus to demonstrate symbols, for example: 6 ? 3 = 18, 18 ? 3 = 6. Can they make up some sums to which they know the answers and give them to a friend? the children could choose the symbols and check with the calculator to see if they have used the right ones.

Cottage loaves The children can use the class shop to reinforce this activity; for example, if buns are 3p each, how many buns for 18p? Let them use real money to solve the problem. Can they get their calculators to agree with their calculations? What operation button did they use?

How quick are you? It is important for the children to realise that the tens are much more important than the units when performing sums. Encourage them to add the tens and then the units. Then they can be encouraged to take away tens one at a time. Tell them to record their answers to enable them to see the emerging pattern.

10p coin take-away The children may like to design a large number square to be displayed. This can be coloured in to show various number patterns and then questions asked, such as. 'Who can count in tens beginning at 14? What about taking away tens beginning at 97?'

Five coins How many different heads and tails patterns were there. How many

arrangements were possible for each one? Do some arrangements produce more patterns than others? Were there any arrangements which produced very few patterns? Display the children's different patterns (arrangements) in a class book.

Telephone cards Please discuss the different ways of recording the results. Did all the ways add up to 10? Why was this? The children can extend this activity to include a take away pattern; that is, if one minute has been used up how many minutes are left and so on? The different patterns could be displayed using a minute time line or 10p coins.

Folding a circle The children could cut out more circles to reproduce and display their results to show how the doubling was achieved. Some of them might like to display the doubling discovered by using calculators.

Change machine Discuss the different arrangements and how they were recorded systematically. The children could design a change machine for use in the class shop. Is a £1 coin the most appropriate and practical value for which to give change – lots of coins may be needed?

Square numbers The children could use large squares of coloured paper to reproduce their patterns with the number of bricks used for each square recorded alongside to show how the squared pattern increases. This display could be used to help with multiplication and division.

Grid games The children can compare their solutions. Were they all the same? Do they notice anything common to all of them? Can they construct their own game where they make a grid containing six odd and three even numbers? Display the grids.

Even-handed Look at the patterns which occur when two numbers are added: an even number to an even number, an odd to an even and an odd to an odd? Make a chart and display it where the children can see it. This should help their arithmetic as well as their understanding of algebra!

Word counts The children can make giant lists or write their words in two large sets. How do they know whether a number is odd or even? What if it is very large? What is the longest word they have found?

Random numbers The children can play this game again in class. Can they place all their numbers in two large sets (use hoops), one for even numbers and one for odd numbers? Discuss how they know if a number is even or odd. What about very large numbers? Can they put some four- or five-digit numbers in their sets?

Adding dice The children can play this again in class, writing down their totals (all of them!). Can they see why it is better to be 'even'? (Even numbers are larger on the dice and will, therefore, lead to a larger score.) What do you get if you add an even number to an even number or an odd to an even number or an odd to an odd? Make a chart and display it where the children can see it. This should help their arithmetic as well as their understanding of algebra!

Spares galore The children can play this again with a grid which they can paste into their maths book or files, colour coding the numbers

in the different times tables. Encourage them to work out which numbers are in which table by counting on. Talk about prime numbers – which will include some they have already covered up (2, 3, 4, 5). Discuss why these are covered.

Counting together! This game leads directly into all the counting together activities which you do with the children 'on the rug' and is immensely beneficial to the children's understanding of how numbers work. Count backwards and forwards, in twos and ones, and then in fives and threes. They should each say a number: point to the person who is to say the next number or go round in turn.

One hundred and seven The children can play this in class in threes and fours – it's quite tricky! Discuss how they know whether a number – particularly a large number – is even or odd. What do they look at?

Answer seven The children can collate all their different sums. How many have they found? How can they be sure they have found them all? Can they make a 'Book of 7' with all the ways of making 7? How about a 'Book of 8' or a 'Book of 6'?

Money madness The children can work in groups and put together all their ways of giving 20p to check that they have found them all. Can they be sure of this? Then they can try to work out how many ways there are of making 10p. Finally, can they work out how many ways there are of making 10 using addition only? (They do not have to be restricted to coin values. For example, 4 + 3 + 3 is a legitimate way of making 10, but not of making 10p!)

Largely odd or even? The children can discuss how they know whether a number is odd or even. What about really large numbers? What are the largest even and odd numbers they can write? How many even numbers are there between 1 and 200?

Odd foods! The children can work in groups and share their information. Which numbers did they generate? How many were even? What sorts of food quantities vary from packet to packet? Which are constant? Move on to discuss which numbers are even and which are odd. How can we tell the difference?

Twenty together The children can make a big display, around a luminous and glowing 20, of all the ways in which 20 can be made. These bonds are very useful when it comes to subtraction, and so knowing what goes with 5 to make 20 is a good way of introducing this. Practice for short periods. 'Six and what make twenty?'

Even time The children can collate all their information. Who was born in a month with an even number of days? Who was born in a month with an odd number of days?

Make a display of their pictures in two sets. Were any children born in a year with an even number of days? Move on to discuss even and odd numbers. How can we tell the difference?

Active and even! The children can make a graph showing all their different numbers of actions. How many hops did they all do? Look at the graph when it is finished and discuss how the children can tell that all the numbers are even. Talk about the difference between even and odd numbers.

Double and win! The children can play the game again in class, writing all their scores in their maths books or files. Discuss why the even person may get a higher score than the odd person. How likely are they to throw an even number or an odd number? Talk about how larger numbers can be even or odd and how we can tell which they are.

Odd cars! The children can discuss the numbers they have found and put them in two lists – even and odd – arranged in size order from the largest to the smallest.

Pair surprise The children can use the cards in class to generate addition sums. What happens if they add two even numbers? Or two odd numbers. What about an even and an odd? Make a chart to demonstrate the outcomes. What about adding the numbers – two evens and one odd and so on?

Five times as much The children can compare amounts. No matter what the starting amount, what do they notice about all the final amounts? Do they need any 2p or 1p coins to give the five-times-as-much score? Why not? Use this activity as a reinforcement of the five times table pattern.

Counting down The children can make a large class spiral, each person writing in a few of the numbers. All the even numbers can be written in red, all the odd in blue. Talk about how we recognise which is which. Test the children out on odd and even numbers between 50 and 100.

Telephone numbers The children can swap over 'sums'. Can they find each other's missing numbers? What happens if two numbers are left out? How many possible solutions are there then? Make a class book of telephone sums.

Coin carve up In class the children can record in a list all the possible amounts. Organise the list so that there is a logic to its ordering. Discuss this logic. If another 1p and 10p were added to the pile, how many more amounts become possible?

The magic rocket

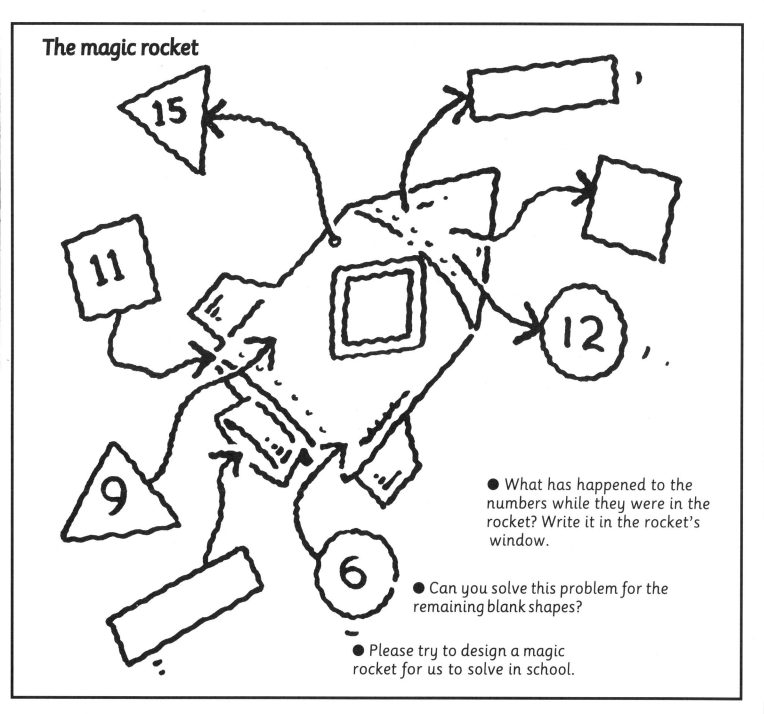

● What has happened to the numbers while they were in the rocket? Write it in the rocket's window.

● Can you solve this problem for the remaining blank shapes?

● Please try to design a magic rocket for us to solve in school.

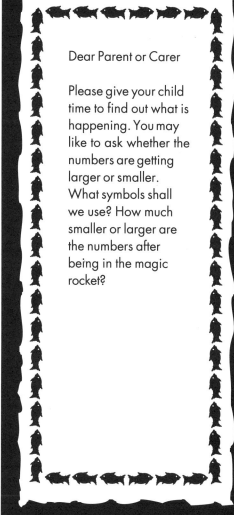
_____and

child

_____

helper(s)

_____

did this activity together

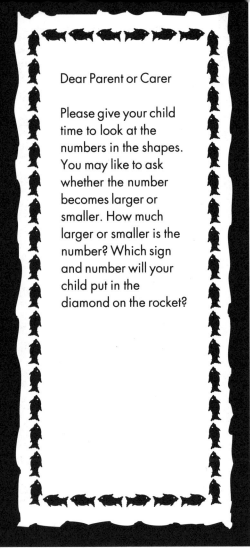
Coming down to Earth

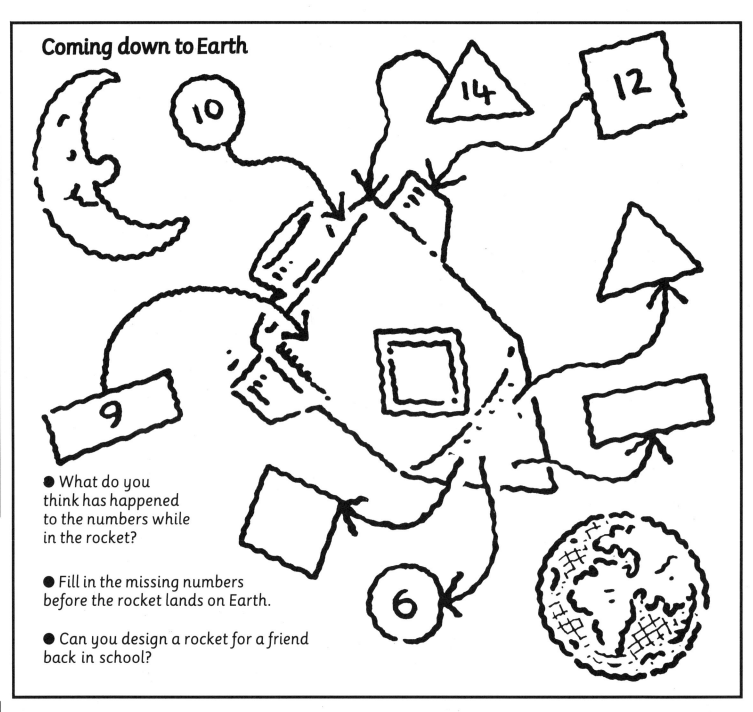

● What do you think has happened to the numbers while in the rocket?

● Fill in the missing numbers before the rocket lands on Earth.

● Can you design a rocket for a friend back in school?

impact MATHS HOMEWORK

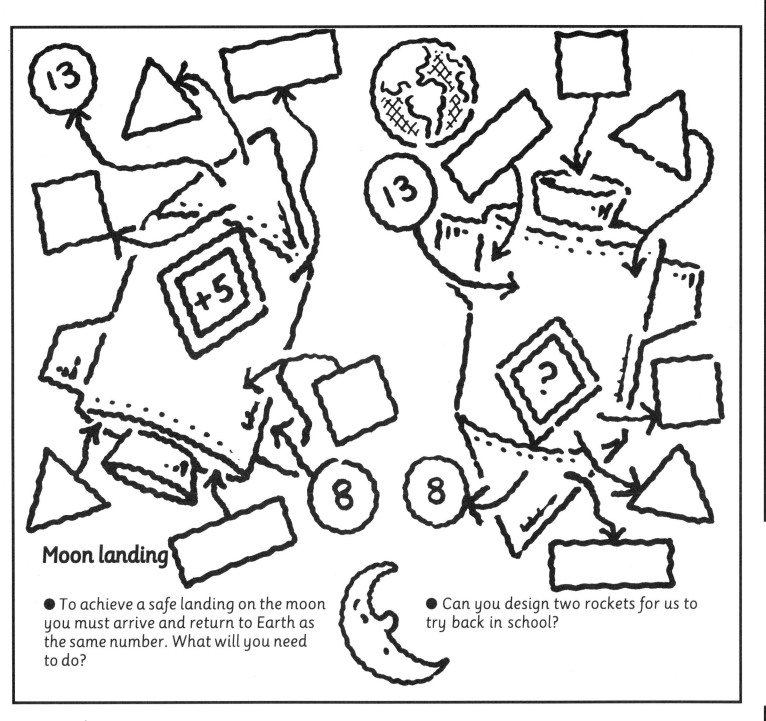

Moon landing

● To achieve a safe landing on the moon you must arrive and return to Earth as the same number. What will you need to do?

● Can you design two rockets for us to try back in school?

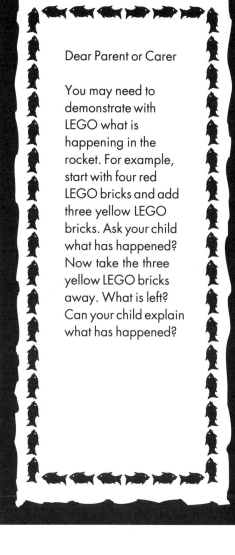

Dear Parent or Carer

You may need to demonstrate with LEGO what is happening in the rocket. For example, start with four red LEGO bricks and add three yellow LEGO bricks. Ask your child what has happened? Now take the three yellow LEGO bricks away. What is left? Can your child explain what has happened?

_____and

child

_____

helper(s)

_____

did this activity together

Cakes

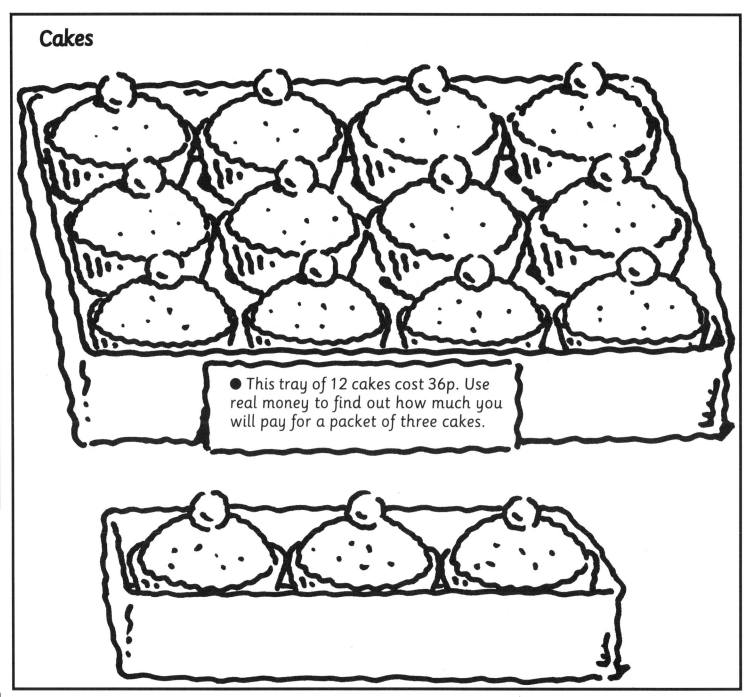

● This tray of 12 cakes cost 36p. Use real money to find out how much you will pay for a packet of three cakes.

impact MATHS HOMEWORK

Halving

● Can you find out half your height?

● How can you solve this problem?

● Bring a piece of string (or a strip of paper) to school that is exactly half your height.

● How long is it?

● How many such strips will fit your height?

Dear Parent or Carer

Please give your child time to investigate different ways of solving this problem.

_____and

child

_____

helper(s)

_____

did this activity together

_____and

child

_____

helper(s)

_____

did this activity together

Halving numbers

● Use LEGO bricks, coins or pasta to help you with this investigation.

● Investigate what happens when you try to divide numbers in half.

● Complete this chart to show which numbers can only be halved once, not at all or more than once.

Number of LEGO bricks	Cannot be halved	Can be halved once	Can be halved again
12		✓	✓

impact MATHS HOMEWORK

Calculator challenge

● Use a calculator to make the following calculation: $3 \times 5 = 15$.

● Can you change 15 back to 3 using only one operation button?

● Which button did you use?

● Investigate some sums for yourself.

● Write a list of your sums and how you changed them back.

● Can you sort your sums into groups or sets? Is there a pattern? Can you explain it?

Dear Parent or Carer

Please give your child time to investigate their own ideas. Investigating our own ideas is a very powerful learning process. Give ideas if your child is becoming frustrated; for example, ask them if the number becomes larger or smaller. 'Can you show me with LEGO how it has become larger?' 'What must you do to return to 15?' 'Now try using the calculator to solve the problem.'

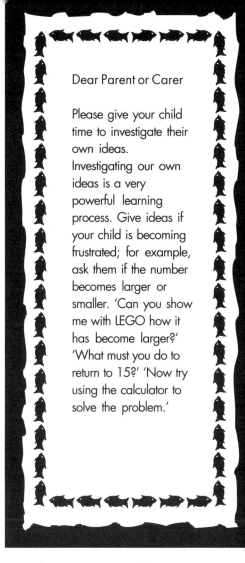

_____and

child

_____

helper(s)

_____

did this activity together

impact MATHS HOMEWORK

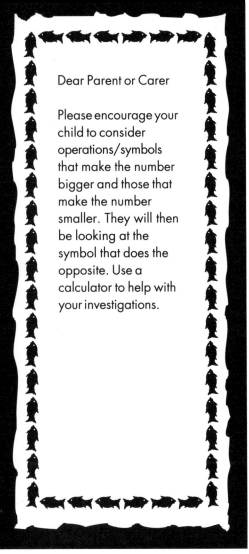
Calculator operations

● Start with 10 and use these operations to find out what happens.

10	×	2	=	
10	–	2	=	
10	+	2	=	
10	÷	2	=	

● Which signs make the number bigger?

● Which signs make the number smaller?

● Try to solve this problem:

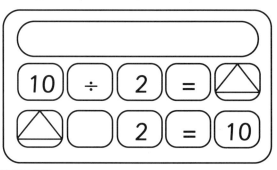

10 ÷ 2 = △

△ ◯ 2 = 10

● Write out below some problems to share with someone at home. Bring your favourite problem back to school to share with the class.

● Can you design a chart to show how the signs work? Use the back of this sheet.

Cottage loaves

● Cottage loaves cost 15p each. They are sold in packets of two. How much does a packet cost?

● PROBLEM: It is the end of the day and the price of each loaf is reduced by 3p. How much does a packet cost now?

● A tray of six loaves costs £1.20. How much for one loaf? How did you find out the answer?

● You can use the back of this sheet to work out your answers.

_____and
child

_____
helper(s)

_____
did this activity together

Dear Parent or Carer

Encourage your child to count the 10p coins first. This activity will encourage mental arithmetic skills. It will also help your child to visualise large numbers.

_____and

child

_____

helper(s)

_____

did this activity together

How quick are you?

YOU WILL NEED: several 10p coins, and a few 5p, 2p and 1p coins.

● Ask someone to play this game with you.

● The first player lays out some of the coins in two sets.

For example:

tens   other coins

● The second player then writes down the total. For example: 35.

● Take turns to lay out some coins.

● Do some sums by adding your sets of coins to your helper's. How many do you have in all?

10p coin take-away

YOU WILL NEED: several 10p coins and a few 2p and 1p coins and the two cards below.

● The first player puts out some coins, 10p coins first. For example:

● The second player writes down the total.

● The first player shows the second player one of the cards (take away 10p or take away 20p). The second player must write down the new answer quickly without touching the coins.

● Check the answers by removing the coins from the pile. Was the second player right?

● Take turns. Are you getting quicker? What do you notice about your answers? Is there a pattern?

● Try changing the cards. You could now write 'Take away 1p coins' and 'Take away 2p coins' on them. Play the game again. Can you see a new pattern?

Take away 10p (subtract)

Take away 20p (subtract)

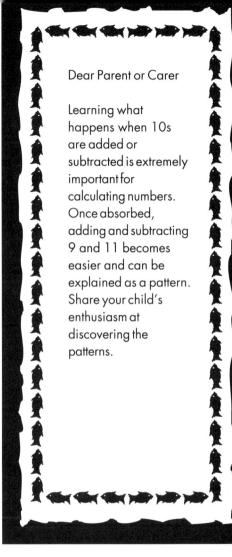

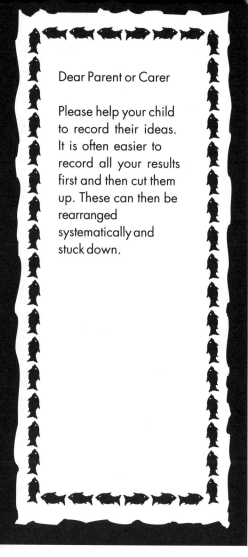
Five coins

YOU WILL NEED: *five coins.*

● Toss the coins in the air and record whether they land heads or tails.

For example:

● Do not turn the coins over again.

● Record in how many different ways you can arrange the heads and tails combination.

● Try and arrange your results systematically.

● Is there a pattern?

● How do you know when you have recorded all the possible patterns (arrangements)?

Telephone cards

- If a £1 telephone card has 10 units and uses 1 unit every minute of talking time (expensive time!), how long would it take to use up the card?

- Find out all the different ways that this time could be used up on two telephone calls?

- Make a record of these different ways.

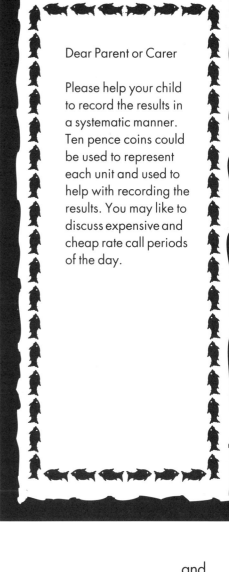

Dear Parent or Carer

Please help your child to record the results in a systematic manner. Ten pence coins could be used to represent each unit and used to help with recording the results. You may like to discuss expensive and cheap rate call periods of the day.

_____and

child

_____

helper(s)

_____

did this activity together

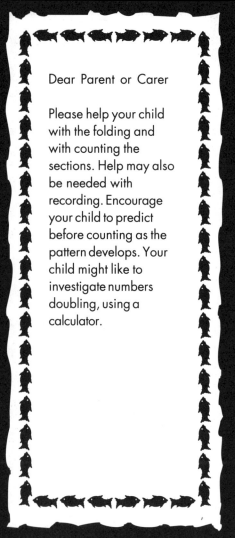

_____and

child

_____

helper(s)

_____

did this activity together

Folding a circle

● Cut out the circle shape on this page.

● Fold your circle in half. How many sections are there?

● Fold it in half again. How many sections are there this time?

● Record the number of folds and the number of sections on your circle. Can you see a pattern?

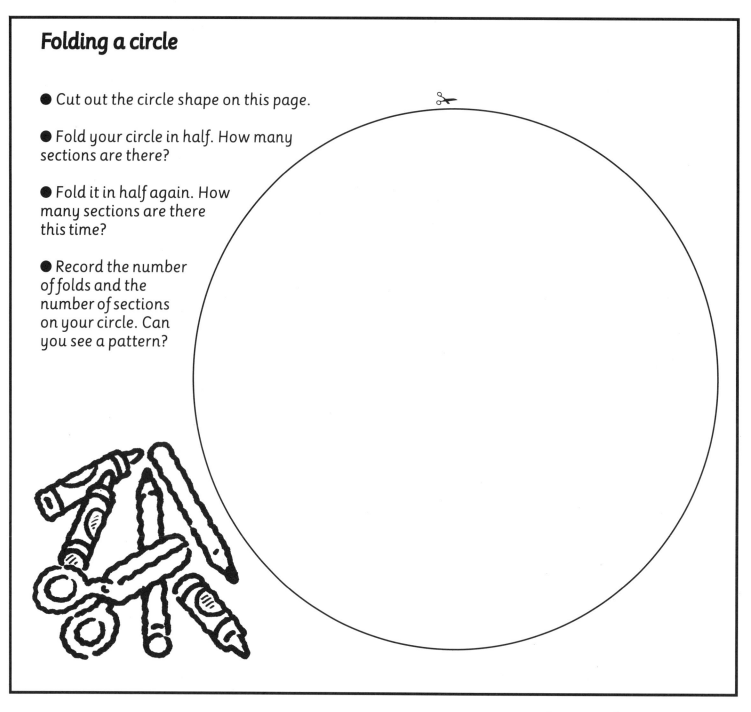

impact MATHS HOMEWORK

Change machine

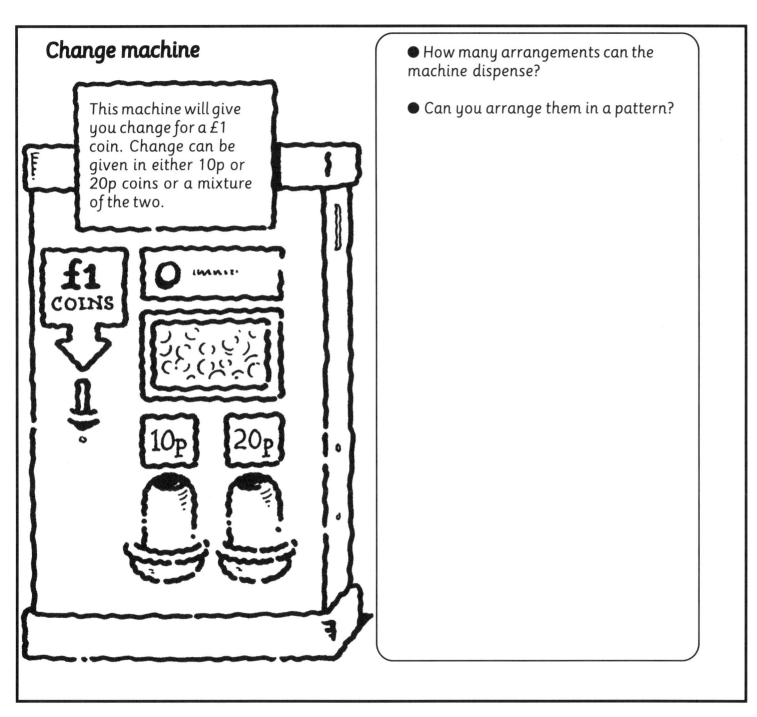

This machine will give you change for a £1 coin. Change can be given in either 10p or 20p coins or a mixture of the two.

£1 COINS

10p   20p

● How many arrangements can the machine dispense?

● Can you arrange them in a pattern?

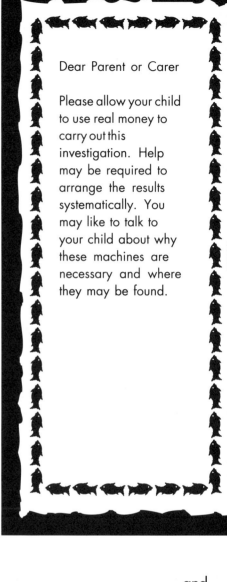
_____and

child

_____

helper(s)

_____

did this activity together

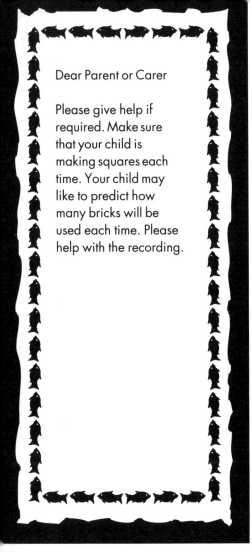
Square numbers

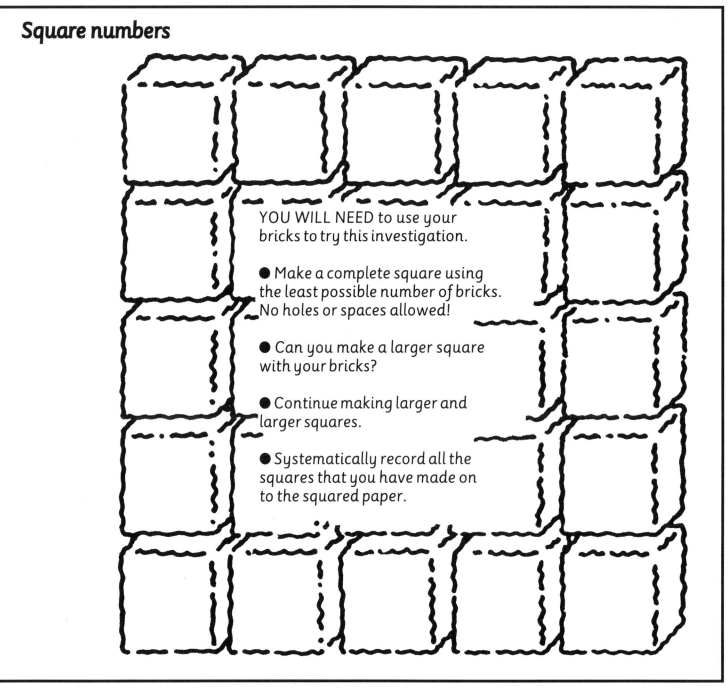

YOU WILL NEED to use your bricks to try this investigation.

● Make a complete square using the least possible number of bricks. No holes or spaces allowed!

● Can you make a larger square with your bricks?

● Continue making larger and larger squares.

● Systematically record all the squares that you have made on to the squared paper.

impact MATHS HOMEWORK

Square numbers

Grid games

● Find someone to work with.

● Look at the grid below.

● Can you rearrange the numbers so that there is one, and only one, odd number in every row and every column?

276	542	661
790	421	863
354	986	778

● Bring your solution into school.

impact MATHS HOMEWORK

Even-handed

YOU WILL NEED: a pile of nuts or raisins or Smarties, and a pencil and paper.

● Take it in turns with someone to grab a large handful of raisins, nuts or Smarties each.

● Guess whether you think you have an even or an odd number.

● Count them.

● If you were right, score 1.

● Now add the handfuls. Will the answer be even or odd? Guess first.

● Work it out or count them all. If you are right, score another point.

● Play until someone has a score of 6 or over.

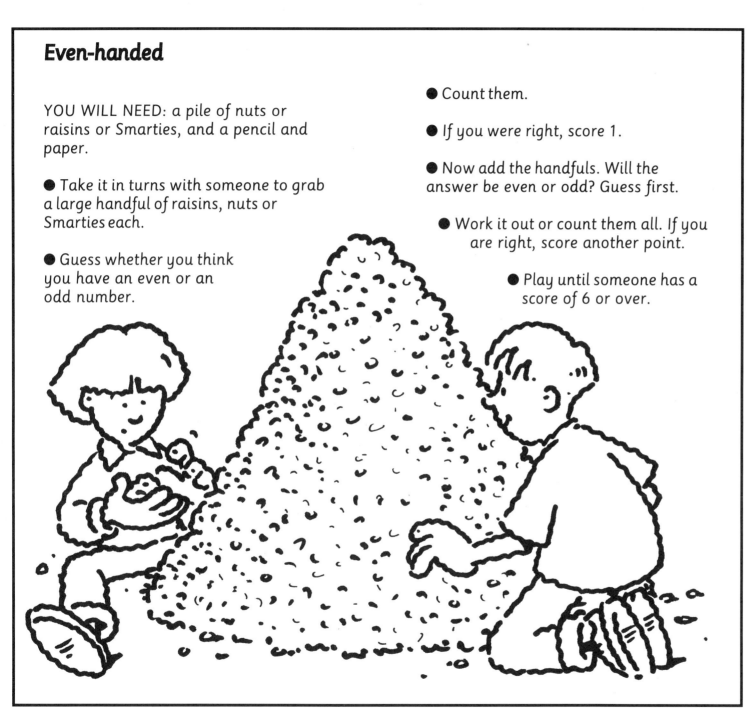

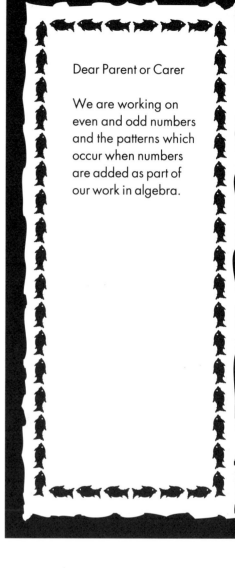

Dear Parent or Carer

We are working on even and odd numbers and the patterns which occur when numbers are added as part of our work in algebra.

_____and
child

_____
helper(s)

_____
did this activity together

Word counts

● Make lists below of your favourite 'even' words and your favourite 'odd' words! That is, words which have an even number of letters or an odd number of letters!

● What is the longest word you can find for each list?

● Bring your lists into school.

impact MATHS HOMEWORK

Random numbers

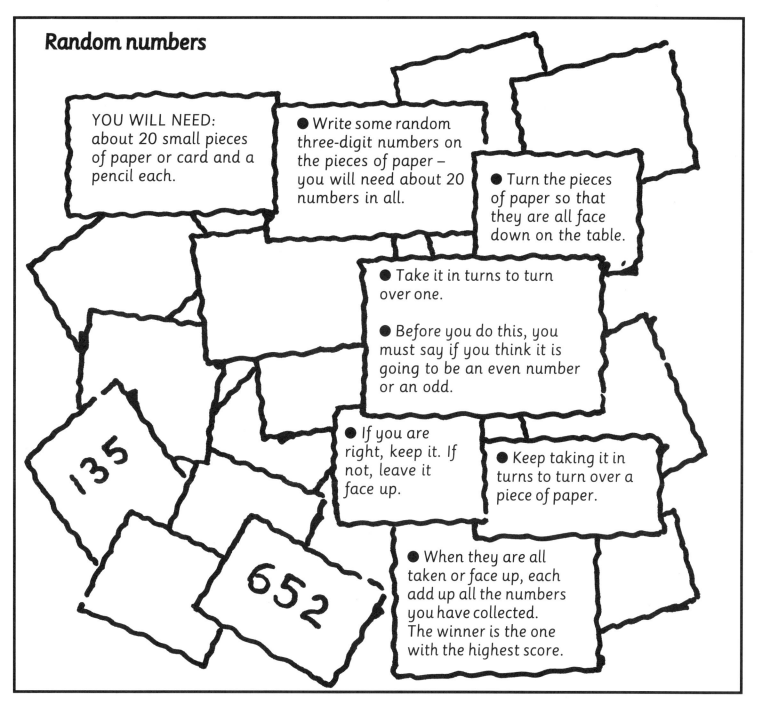

YOU WILL NEED: about 20 small pieces of paper or card and a pencil each.

● Write some random three-digit numbers on the pieces of paper – you will need about 20 numbers in all.

● Turn the pieces of paper so that they are all face down on the table.

● Take it in turns to turn over one.

● Before you do this, you must say if you think it is going to be an even number or an odd.

● If you are right, keep it. If not, leave it face up.

● Keep taking it in turns to turn over a piece of paper.

● When they are all taken or face up, each add up all the numbers you have collected. The winner is the one with the highest score.

impact MATHS HOMEWORK

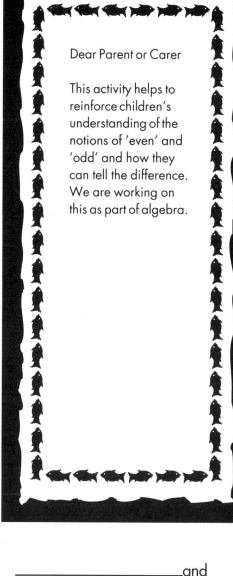

Dear Parent or Carer

This activity helps to reinforce children's understanding of the notions of 'even' and 'odd' and how they can tell the difference. We are working on this as part of algebra.

_____and

child

_____

helper(s)

_____

did this activity together

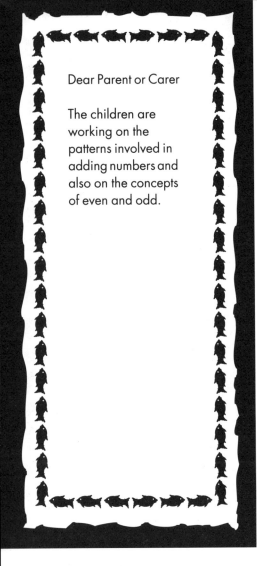

_____and

child

_____

helper(s)

_____

did this activity together

Adding dice

YOU WILL NEED: a dice and a pencil and paper.

● Decide which of you is going to collect 'even' totals and which of you is going to collect 'odd' totals.

● Take it in turns to throw the dice twice. Add the totals.

● If the answer is even and you are collecting even totals, you may score that number.

● If it is odd and you are collecting odd totals you may score it.

● Otherwise no score!

● Keep playing until someone gets a score of over 24.

● Play several times. Is it better to be 'even' or 'odd'?

impact MATHS HOMEWORK

Spares galore

YOU WILL NEED: a dice, a pencil, and a pile of counters, small bricks or dried pasta.

● Use the grid below.

1	2	3	4	5	6
7	8	9	10	11	12
13	14	15	16	17	18
19	20	21	22	23	24
25	26	27	28	29	30
31	32	33	34	35	36

● Take it in turns to throw the dice.

● Place a counter on the grid on any number which is in the times table of the number thrown. For example, if you throw a 4, place a counter on the grid on any number in the four times table.

● Keep playing until someone throws a number where all the possible squares for that number are covered. Then that player must keep the counter.

● Play until there are no possible spaces on the grid at all.

● Which numbers are still uncovered?

● Draw a ring around these on the grid.

● The winner is the person with the fewest counters in their possession.

● Bring your grid back into school.

Dear Parent or Carer

This game leads into our work on number patterns and prime numbers. This is all part of the study of algebra.

_____and

child

_____

helper(s)

_____

did this activity together

_____and
child

_____
helper(s)

_____
did this activity together

Counting together!

● Have you ever tried counting together? You take it in turns to say the numbers.

For example: I start with, 'One!', and you say, 'Two', and then I continue with, 'Three' and so on.

● Find someone to play with. First try easy counting, each saying alternate numbers.

● See how fast and how accurately you can do this. It is harder than you imagine!

● Now try some harder counting. Count in twos starting with 1. Thus, 'One', 'Three', 'Five', 'Seven' and so on.

● Try counting backwards in twos from 30.

● Try counting in threes or in fives.

● See how good you can get!

impact MATHS HOMEWORK

One hundred and seven

● One of you is 'even' and one of you is 'odd'.

● Take it in turns to say a number out loud.

● If you are 'even', it must be an even number. If you are 'odd', it must be an odd number.

● The number you say must be higher than the number said before you.

For example: if I say 3 to start off (I'm 'odd' numbers!) then you might say 4, or 14 or 22, but you may not say 2 (because that is smaller than 3).

● The first person to say either 107 or a number bigger than that is the loser.

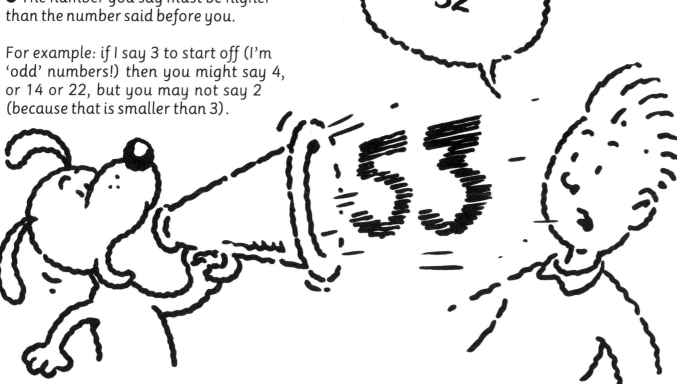

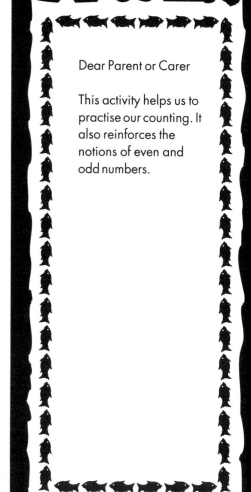

Dear Parent or Carer

This activity helps us to practise our counting. It also reinforces the notions of even and odd numbers.

_____and
child

_____
helper(s)

_____

did this activity together

impact MATHS HOMEWORK

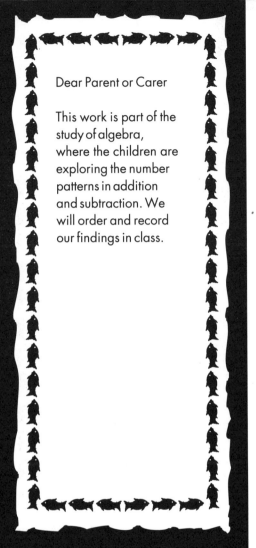

_____and

child

_____

helper(s)

_____

did this activity together

Answer seven

● How many sums can you make up which all have the answer 7?

● You may only use adding up and whole numbers.

So, one sum could be:

1 + 1 + 1 + 1 + 1 + 1 + 1

= 7

● How many sums can you make up? Write them in the seven outline opposite. Are they all different?

● Bring all your sums into school.

impact MATHS HOMEWORK

Money madness

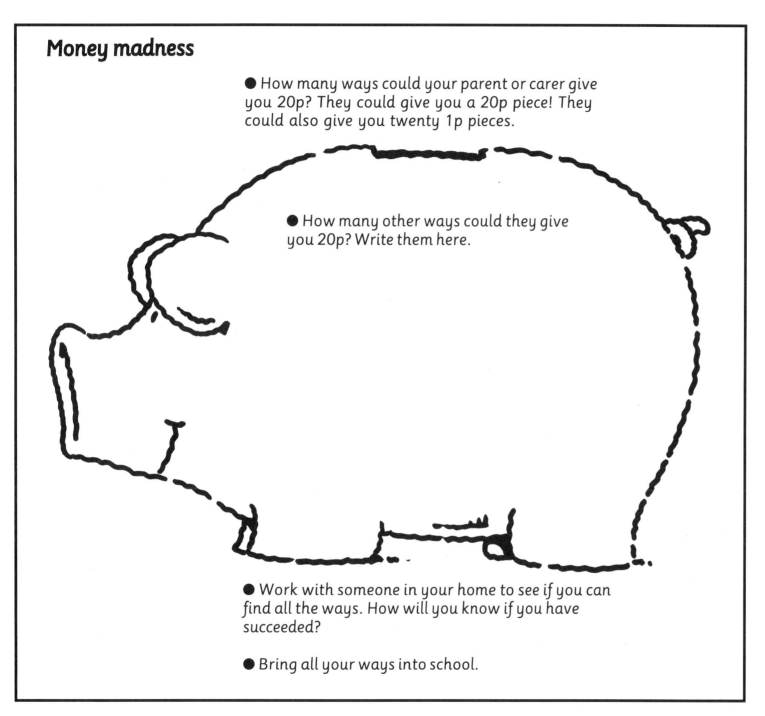

● How many ways could your parent or carer give you 20p? They could give you a 20p piece! They could also give you twenty 1p pieces.

● How many other ways could they give you 20p? Write them here.

● Work with someone in your home to see if you can find all the ways. How will you know if you have succeeded?

● Bring all your ways into school.

Dear Parent or Carer

This activity helps children to think about the patterns involved in adding numbers, and also about how to organise and record their data.

_____and

child

_____

helper(s)

_____

did this activity together

Largely odd or even?

● Are there more odd numbers or more even numbers?

● Imagine that you have written a book. It has 100 pages. Just before it is due to be printed the person publishing it tells you that their machine has gone wrong and that they cannot print any odd page numbers.

● How many pages will be affected?

● Would it be better if it was the even numbers that had gone wrong?

6

impact MATHS HOMEWORK

Odd foods!

● Is food usually packaged in even numbers or odd numbers of items?

● This weekend, check out as many packets and bags of things as you can.

● Do packets of biscuits contain an even or an odd number of biscuits?

● What about packets of crisps? Or sliced loaves of bread?

● Check out as many different sorts of food as you can and bring all your information into school.

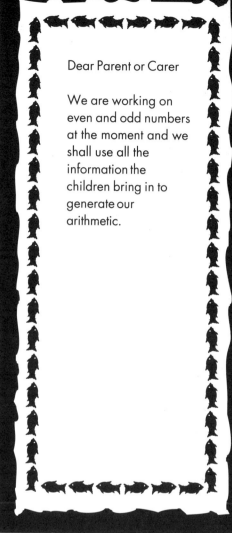

_____and

child

_____

helper(s)

_____

did this activity together

impact MATHS HOMEWORK

Twenty together

● In this sum, the cat and the dog stand for numbers:

● How many different numbers can each one be to make the sum work?

impact MATHS HOMEWORK

Even time

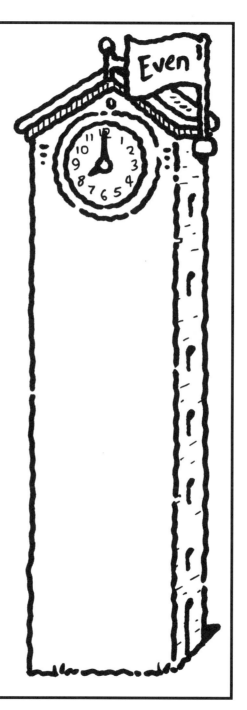

● For how many hours in the day does the clock strike an even number of times? For how many does it strike an odd number?

● How many months of the year have an even number of days? How many have an odd number?

● Which years have an even number of days in them?

● Write all the things that you can think of to do with time on the appropriate clock.

● Bring your lists into school.

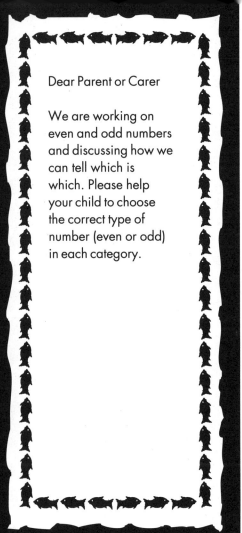

_____ and

child

_____

helper(s)

_____

did this activity together

Active and even!

● Find someone to help you, and do the following actions:

  • an even number of hops (on one leg!);

  • an odd number of jumps;

  • an even number of hand-claps;

  • an odd number of throws of a soft ball, or a teddy, into the air;

  • an even number of bunny hops;

  • an odd number of cat or dog noises!

● Ask your helper to write down how many you did of each.

● Bring your sheet back into school.

impact MATHS HOMEWORK

Double and win!

YOU WILL NEED: a dice and a piece of paper and a pencil.

● With someone in your house, decide who is going to be 'even' and who is going to be 'odd'.

● Take it in turns to throw the dice.

● Score the number you throw. BUT if you are 'even', and the number that you throw is 'even', you may score DOUBLE that number.

● Similarly, if the number you throw is 'odd' and you are the 'odd' person, you may score DOUBLE the number thrown.

● Play until either the even person gets a score of 100 or the odd person gets a score of 75.

● Why does the even person have to get more than the odd person to win?

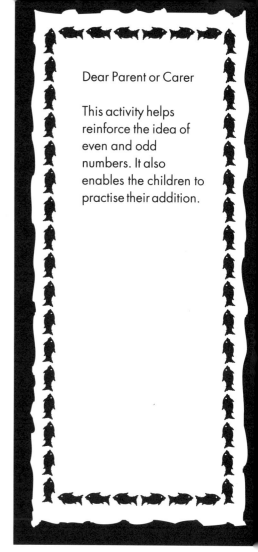

Dear Parent or Carer

This activity helps reinforce the idea of even and odd numbers. It also enables the children to practise their addition.

_____and

child

_____

helper(s)

_____

did this activity together

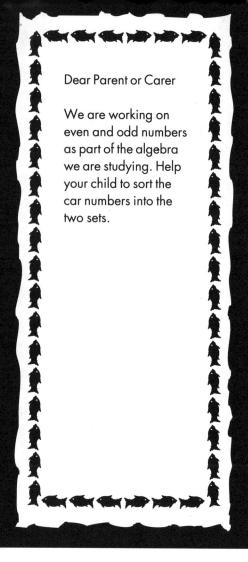

_____and

child

_____

helper(s)

_____

did this activity together

Odd cars!

YOU WILL NEED: a pencil and paper.

● With someone to help you, write down as many car registration numbers as you can.

● Now sort them into these two sets – even numbers and odd numbers.

● Discuss how you know which is which.

● Bring both your sets into school.

ODD

EVEN

impact MATHS HOMEWORK

Pair surprise

YOU WILL NEED: a pack of cards with the face (picture) cards removed.

● Deal out three cards to yourself and three to your helper.

● Look at your cards. Find two cards which add up to an even number and place them down in front of you.

● The person whose cards make the highest score takes all four cards and piles them up beside them.

● Then each take two more cards from the pack.

● This time you have to select two cards which make an odd number. Both put your pairs down in front of you.

● Keep playing, alternating between even and odd numbers.

● The first person to collect eight pairs is the winner.

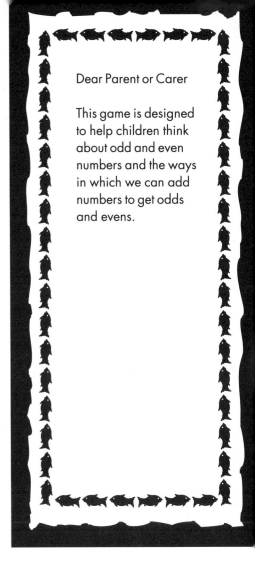

_____and

child

_____

helper(s)

_____

did this activity together

_____and

child

_____

helper(s)

_____

did this activity together

Five times as much

● Ask a grown-up in your home to empty their pockets of all their change. Tell them that you will let them have it all back!

● Count how much they have!

● Write it down.

● Now you are going to work out how much they would have if they had five times as much!

● Multiply each of the coins in turn by five and write down the answers.

● Add up all your answers.

● How much would they have?

● On the back of the sheet, draw the notes and coins they would have if they had this much money!

impact MATHS HOMEWORK

Counting down

● The spiral on the snail's shell has all the odd numbers from 1–60 in it. Fill in those that are missing.

● Draw your own shape with all the even numbers in it above.

Dear Parent or Carer

This activity helps to reinforce the idea of odd and even numbers. Help your child with the missing numbers. How can we tell if a number is even or odd?

_____and

child

_____

helper(s)

_____

did this activity together

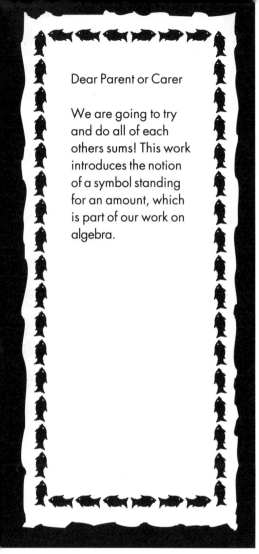
_____and

child

_____

helper(s)

_____

did this activity together

Telephone sums

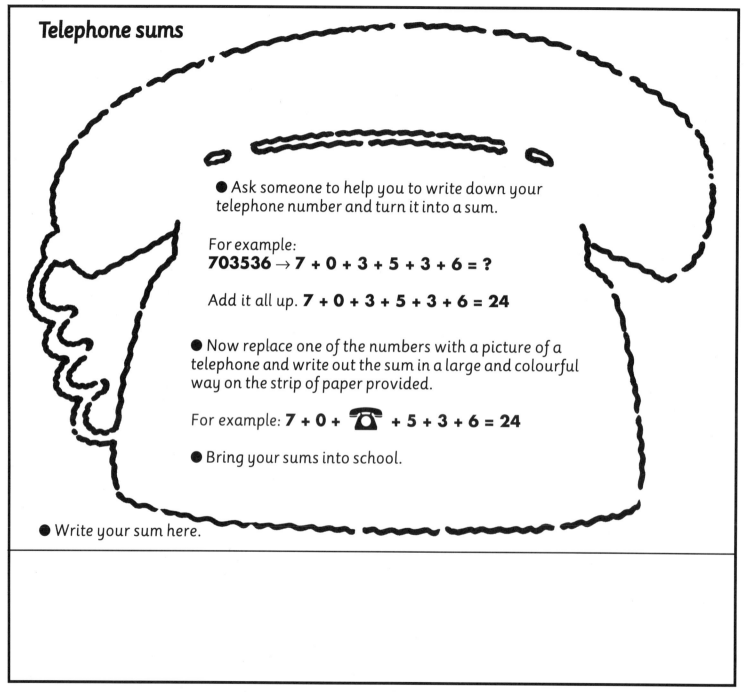

● Ask someone to help you to write down your telephone number and turn it into a sum.

For example:
703536 → 7 + 0 + 3 + 5 + 3 + 6 = ?

Add it all up. **7 + 0 + 3 + 5 + 3 + 6 = 24**

● Now replace one of the numbers with a picture of a telephone and write out the sum in a large and colourful way on the strip of paper provided.

For example: **7 + 0 + ☎ + 5 + 3 + 6 = 24**

● Bring your sums into school.

● Write your sum here.

Coin carve-up

YOU WILL NEED: four 10p, two 2p and two 1p coins, a pencil and a piece of paper.

● Using some or all of the coins and NO OTHERS, how many different amounts of money can you make?

● Which amounts between 44p and 1p is it impossible to make?

● Write down all the possible amounts in the money bag below!

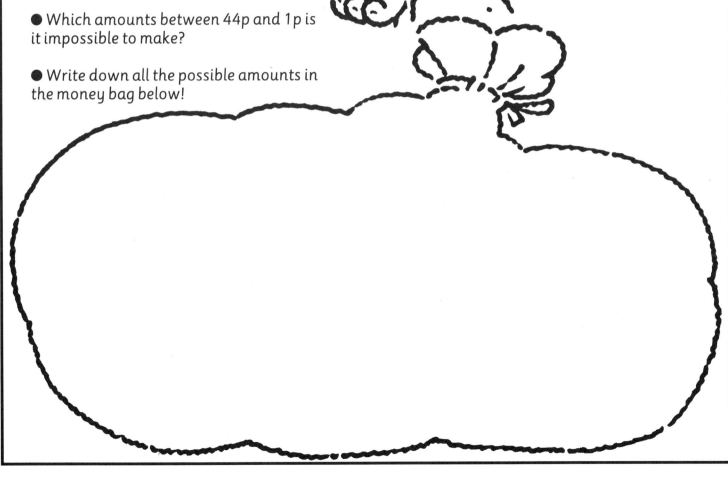

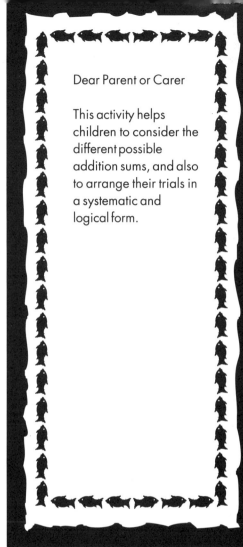

Dear Parent or Carer

This activity helps children to consider the different possible addition sums, and also to arrange their trials in a systematic and logical form.

_____and

child

_____

helper(s)

_____

did this activity together

Scottish National Guidelines Mathematics 5–14

Number, Money and Measurement

Patterns and Sequences

Level A – Work with patterns and sequences; simple number sequences; copy, continue and describe simple patterns or sequences of objects of different shape or colour.

Level B – Work with patterns and sequences; even and odd numbers; whole number sequences within 100; more complex sequences with shapes.

Level C – Work with patterns and relationships within and among multiplication tables.

Functions and Equations

Level B – Find the missing numbers in statements where symbols are used for unknown numbers or operators.

Level C – Use a simple 'function machine' for operations involving doubling, halving, adding and subtracting.

Northern Ireland Programme of Study for Mathematics at Key Stage 1

Number

Understanding number and number notation

Pupils should have opportunities to:

a count orally, knowing the number names, initially working with small numbers; count collections of objects and know that the size of a set is given by the last number in the count; understand the empty set and the conservation of number;

b read, write and order whole numbers, initially to 10, progressing to at least 1000; use the knowledge that the position of a digit indicates its value;

c make a sensible estimate of a small number of objects; begin to approximate to the nearest 10 or 100;

d recognise and use simple everyday fractions and their notation in practical situations.

Patterns, relationships and sequences

Pupils should have opportunities to:

a copy, continue and devise repeating patterns; distinguish between odd and even numbers;

b explore and record addition and subtraction patterns and patterns in number tables; explaining and using them to make predictions, initially working with number patterns up to 20 and then to 100; progress to exploring multiplication and division patterns;

c understand the commutative property of addition and the relationship between addition and subtraction;

d understand the use of a symbol to stand for an unknown number;

e understand and use simple function machines.